DATE DUE

DEMCO, INC. 38-2931

THE STORY OF
FOOTBALL

THE STORY OF
FOOTBALL

DAVE ANDERSON

FOREWORD BY O.J. SIMPSON

WILLIAM MORROW AND COMPANY, INC.
New York

Library of Congress Cataloging in Publication Data
Anderson, Dave.   The story of football.
Includes index. 1. Football—United States—History. I. Title.
GV950.A53 1985   796.332'0973   85-7195
ISBN 0-688-05634-2
ISBN 0-688-05635-0 (pbk.)

THE STORY OF
FOOTBALL

FOREWORD

While I was learning to play football, I always thought that it was equally important to learn how football began in the United States and how it developed into the great game it is today. During the time I was growing up in San Francisco, the best football player in the NFL was Jim Brown, the Cleveland Browns' fullback. He was what I wanted to be—the NFL's best running back. As it turned out, my dream came true. I broke his NFL rushing record in 1973, just as Eric Dickerson of the Los Angeles Rams broke my record in 1984.

But for me to understand that Jim Brown had been the best at that time, I had to know about the great players before him, going all the way back to Jim Thorpe, the 1912 Olympic decathlon champion, who was one of the roots of pro football.

In writing *The Story of Football,* Dave Anderson introduces you to all the famous players and coaches, as well as to football's fundamentals—rushing, passing, pass-receiving, kicking, blocking, defense. There's even a chapter on coaching.

But what I like best about the book is that it gives you a sense of what football is, why people like to play it, and why just about everyone likes to watch it—the action. That's what I enjoyed.

Every time I carried the ball, I was in the middle of the action. My teammates were blocking for me. And I was trying to get as many yards as I could. I wanted to score a touchdown for my team every time. I didn't score every time, of course, but that's what I hoped to do. And that's what every player should try to do on every play—help his team score a touchdown.

The Story of Football also explains why teamwork is so important. If a team doesn't play together, it just won't be a winner.

When I was voted the Heisman Trophy at the University of Southern California, and then when I set the NFL rushing record while playing with the Buffalo Bills, it was my name in most of the headlines. But without my teammates blocking for me, I wouldn't have gotten that far.

All that action and teamwork is here in *The Story of Football,* a book for everyone. I'm sure you'll learn something about this wonderful game. I know I did.

O. J. Simpson

CONTENTS

PART ONE

Football at its best on offense and defense: even when in the grasp of a tackler, Jim Brown often powered his way to extra yardage.

IN THE BEGINNING

"All Football Comes from Stagg"

Lamar Hunt couldn't believe it. His daughter Sharon had just bounced a small red, white, and blue ball over the roof of their home into their backyard.

"What's that?" he asked.

"A super ball. That's its real name, Daddy, super ball."

"It sure bounces super."

Hunt, the owner of the Kansas City Chiefs, didn't realize it at the time, but that high-bouncing hard-rubber ball would inspire the name of football's most important game. After the 1966 merger agreement between the National Football League (NFL) and the American Football League (AFL), a championship game was scheduled for the two titleholders.

"In our discussions, we kept referring to it as the 'final game' or the 'championship game' or whatever, but it was awkward," Hunt has recalled. "One day I happened to say, 'When we get to the super bowl . . .' and everyone knew what I was talking about. The term must have come from that 'super ball' my daughter had."

In time the NFL adopted "Super Bowl" as the official name for its championship game.

Now, year after year, Super Bowl games are listed by Roman numerals, as if ordained for history. More than a hundred thousand spectators have filled a huge stadium for this championship game of the National Football League; more than a hundred million people have watched it on television. In college football the New Year's Day bowl games entertain America on TV for nearly twelve continuous hours. High school games unite small towns and neighborhoods of big cities. And in their own backyards little boys grow up throwing a football, pretending to be the latest popular quarterback.

This is the spectacle of the game as we know it today. But in the beginning, as with all our sports, football's roots were small, its appeal limited, its appearance almost ancient.

Half a century before the NFL was organized in 1920, on November 6, 1869, at New Brunswick, New Jersey, teams from Rutgers and Princeton played what historians consider to be the first college football game. The rules ordered "no throwing or running with the round inflated ball," but it could be batted or dribbled. More of a soccer game than a football game, it attracted about one hundred spectators, along with the twenty-five players on each team, to a grassy field where a Rutgers gymnasium would stand one hundred years later.

To identify themselves, the Rutgers players, along with about fifty students, wore scarlet-colored scarves wrapped turban-style around their heads. Rutgers teams in all sports now are known as the Scarlet Knights.

"To appreciate this first game to the full, you must know something of its background," one of the original Rutgers players, John W. Herbert, wrote: "The two colleges were, and still are, of course, about twenty miles apart. The rivalry between them was intense. For years each had striven for possession of an old Revolutionary cannon, making night forays and lugging it back and forth time and again. Not long before the first football game, the canny Princetonians had settled this competition in their own favor by ignominiously sinking the gun in several feet of concrete."

After issuing the challenge for the first football game, Rutgers won, 6–4, with the points scored one at a time on kicks that went

When Princeton played Cornell in 1903, helmets were not mandatory.

over the goal line, not through uprights. In a rematch a week later Princeton won, 8–0. Originally a third game had been scheduled, but the faculties of both institutions ordered it cancelled. The games, the administrations agreed, had been interfering with the players' studies. After only two games college football was faced with its first accusation of athletic "overemphasis"—a problem that would evolve along with the sport itself.

The following year Columbia organized a football team that played both Rutgers and Princeton using the soccer-type rules of the time.

Although there were no college games recorded during the 1871 season, Yale played its first game the next year, defeating Columbia, 30–0. And in 1874 the transition from soccer to football began. Harvard, which had organized a team the previous fall but had not been able to schedule an opponent, invited McGill University of Montreal, Canada, to send its football team to Cambridge, Massachusetts, for a May 15 game. But when the McGill team warmed up, its players were running with the ball.

"What game are you playing?" the Harvard captain asked.

"Rugby," the McGill captain said. "Rugby is our game."

"Our game is soccer—kicking the ball," the Harvard captain said. "Our rules don't allow us to run with the ball. But you are our guests. We will play under your rules."

"No," the McGill captain said, "we will play one game under your rules, one game under our rules."

Although the game played under rugby rules ended in a 0–0 tie, Harvard's players clearly preferred those rules. The next year, on November 13, 1875, the Harvard team traveled to New Haven, Connecticut, to play Yale for the first time. Again the rules

The faces aren't any different from today's players, but the uniforms are. (Princeton, 1890)

created some confusion until Yale, always a proper host, agreed to play a game more like rugby than soccer. Yale lost 4–0, but football, as we know it now, had really begun.

The next year Yale, having adopted the rugby style, won, 1–0, with a freshman named Walter Camp, who would later compete on six Yale football teams under that era's casual eligibility rules. Camp later became a Yale coach and the most famous All-America team selector. For several decades the highest honor in college football was to be chosen on Walter Camp's All-America team.

Harvard would not defeat Yale again until 1890, by which time the first American football rules had been devised—downs, yards to gain, tackling below the waist, blocking, 4 points for a touchdown (not 6 points as it is now). Also that year Harvard was serious enough about football to institute spring practice. Three years later the Harvard Crimson wore slippery leather uniforms instead of cloth.

During those years, "The Game," as the Harvard-Yale rivalry is

Philbin of Yale bursting through Harvard's line in their 1907 game.

known now in the East, was played at a neutral site—Springfield, Massachusetts. Special trains would arrive from Boston and New Haven, Connecticut, and organized cheering would explode from the standing-room-only crowds. One of the earliest mascots, the first real Yale bulldog, Handsome Dan, waddled onto the sidelines at Springfield in the first game there.

Yale, Harvard, and Princeton—still known as the Big Three—dominated college football along with the University of Pennsylvania in those early years. But as the twentieth century began, this new American game also was being played at colleges across the land.

The first important American coach was Amos Alonzo Stagg, who devoted himself to football after having been an All-America end in 1889. Stagg was a Yale divinity student, but instead of becoming a minister, he began coaching in 1890 at Springfield (Massachusetts) College, then moved in 1892 to the University of Chicago, where he would remain through the 1932 season. Although he was forced into mandatory retirement there at age seventy, he was still eager to coach. Stagg was hired the next year by the University of the Pacific in Stockton, California. He happened to travel to his new job on a train that President Herbert Hoover was on.

"When the train got there," one of his sons recalled later, "there were hundreds of people at the station. He assumed that they were there to see the President, but they were there to greet him."

By then Stagg was revered as a coach who had shaped the game of football as we know it now. He is credited by some historians with having pioneered the forward pass, the T-formation, the single and double flanker, the huddle, the shift, the man-in-motion, the quick kick, the short kickoff, and the short punt formation. On a field goal, he used a placekick rather than a drop-kick. He invented uniform numbers, the tackling dummy, the blocking sled, padded goalposts, and to the agony of players everywhere, wind sprints.

"All football," the famous Notre Dame coach Knute Rockne would later say, "comes from Stagg."

Stagg died in 1965 at the age of 102, but he had established the college record of 314 victories that Paul (Bear) Bryant surpassed as the University of Alabama coach and that Eddie Robinson surpassed as the Grambling coach. Stagg won 244 games at Chicago, 60 at Pacific, and 10 at Springfield.

Other coaches also influenced the game, notably Glenn (Pop) Warner, for whom America's most popular boys' football league is named.

Praised by Stagg as "one of football's excellent creators," Warner invented the single wing and the double wing formations, along with such plays as the reverse, the naked reverse, the crouching start, the rolling block, the unbalanced line, the screen pass, and the hidden-ball play. He also devised the spiral punt, the numbering of plays, and fiber padding, which evolved into today's sturdy plastic helmets and other protective equipment. Beginning in 1895 at Georgia, Warner went on to coach at Cornell, the Carlisle Indian School, the University of Pittsburgh, Stanford, and Temple.

Warner's teams won 313 games, one fewer than Stagg's total, with a philosophy that concentrated on serious practice.

"You play the way you practice," he once said. "Practice the right way, and you will react the right way in a game."

Inspired by Stagg's championship teams at Chicago, Michigan put together one of the most powerful teams around the turn of the century. Its 1901 team had an 11–0 record, outscoring its opponents, 550–0, and winning the first Rose Bowl game at Pasadena, California, on New Year's Day 1902, with a 49–0 rout of Stanford.

Amos Alonzo Stagg, the first important American football coach.

"In 1901," the Michigan coach, Fielding (Hurry Up) Yost, later said, "we used spinners, reverses, double reverses, laterals, split backs—everything that is in the modern game except the forward pass."

Yost got his "Hurry Up" nickname from the quickness he demanded of his team in running the next play. As soon as one play ended, the Michigan quarterback, Boss Weeks, would be calling signals while the opposing tacklers were dragging themselves to their feet and returning to the line of scrimmage.

Another important coach was John Heisman, who spread the gospel of football throughout the nation, starting before the turn of the century and on into the 1920s.

Heisman, for whom the trophy now honoring the nation's outstanding college player is named, moved all over the country—Oberlin, Akron, Clemson, University of Pennsylvania, Washington and Jefferson, Rice, and Georgia Tech. In his later years he was the athletic director at the Downtown Athletic Club in New York City, the club that sponsors the Heisman Trophy balloting.

Meanwhile the game's rules were changing almost year to year, as administrators and coaches sought to develop a balance between offensive and defensive football as well as protection from injuries.

In the process the first pro football player appeared. William (Pudge) Heffelfinger had been an All-America guard at Yale in 1889, 1890, and 1891. The following year he was playing for the Chicago Athletic Association when he was offered five hundred dollars by the Allegheny Athletic Association team to appear at Pittsburgh in a November 12 game against the rival Pittsburgh Athletic Club. Midway in the first half, Heffelfinger recovered a

John Heisman (*right*), the Pennsylvania coach for whom the Heisman
Trophy is named, chats with Assistant Coach F. Harold Gaston in 1922.

fumble and ran 25 yards for the game's only touchdown in the 4–0 victory.

"Game performance bonus," the Allegheny team's financial statement read, "to W. Heffelfinger for playing: (cash) $500."

With that payment, professional football had begun. Football itself had outgrown its infancy. It was ready for its adolescence and, eventually, for maturity.

1900-1930

Jim Thorpe and Knute Rockne

On a dusty dirt field in Canton, Ohio, in 1915, the Canton Bulldogs with Jim Thorpe were playing the rival Massillon Tigers with Knute Rockne. The two most famous players of that era, Thorpe was a bruising running back and Rockne was a determined defensive end when he wasn't catching passes. On one play Rockne broke through to tackle Thorpe for no gain. Not long after that, Rockne again tackled Thorpe for no gain. But the next time Thorpe carried the ball, he slammed past Rockne for several yards. On his way back to the huddle, Thorpe spoke to Rockne. Two versions of that encounter have drifted down.

According to one version, Thorpe is supposed to have said, "That was just a warning, Rock. People came here and paid to see Jim run. You better let Jim run."

As told by Rockne himself, the other version, is: "Jim never actually said it that way. It was more like, 'I'm glad you're slowing down, Rock. Now the people who're paying to see me run can get their money's worth.'"

Whatever was said that day, Jim Thorpe and Knute Rockne created the headlines that popularized football long before television was invented.

Jim Thorpe, who was told, "You, sir, are the greatest athlete in the world."

Thorpe, an American Indian from the Sac and Fox tribe in Oklahoma, was a running back at the Carlisle (Pennsylvania) Institute, a vocational school operated by the federal government for Indian students. Rockne, a Norwegian immigrant who grew up in Chicago, was the Notre Dame end whose pass catching led to the adoption of the forward pass as a strategic weapon. Rockne remained at Notre Dame as one of college football's most famous coaches until his death in 1931 in a plane crash.

Thorpe was more than a football player. He is considered to have been one of the world's outstanding all-around athletes. At the 1912 Olympics in Stockholm, he won gold medals in both the decathlon and pentathlon.

The decathlon consists of ten events, then spread over three days instead of the current two days: the 100-meter dash, long jump, shot put, high jump, 400-meter run, discus, 110-meter hurdles, pole vault, javelin, and 1,500-meter run. The pentathlon, which has been replaced in the Olympics by the modern pentathlon, originally had these five events: 200-meter dash, 1,500-meter run, long jump, discus, and javelin. As he stood on the victory stand, Thorpe was presented his two gold medals by King Gustaf V of Sweden.

"You, sir," the king said, "are the greatest athlete in the world."

In the United States, tackles who had tried to stop Jim Thorpe and athletes who had tried to run and jump against him agreed with King Gustaf V's assessment. James Francis Thorpe and his twin brother Charles were born on May 28, 1888, in a cabin on the Sac and Fox reservation near Bellemont in the Oklahoma Territory, as it was known before statehood. James also had an Indian name given him by his mother that morning as she noticed the sun on the path to her cabin.

"Wa-tho-huk," she called him, meaning "Bright Path."

As a youngster, Jim attended the Haskell Institute in Oklahoma, where he first competed in football, baseball, and track-and-field. When he was sixteen, he arrived at Carlisle, where Pop Warner was the football coach. Thorpe played football there in 1907 and 1908, then rejoined the team for the 1911 season. Despite its small enrollment—it was more of a vocational school than a college—Carlisle played some of the nation's best college teams. On November 11, 1911, the Indians were in Cambridge to oppose Harvard, perhaps the best team of that era. From 1908 through 1916, the Crimson had a 71–7–5 record under Coach Percy Haughton, including 33 consecutive victories.

Harvard took a 6–0 lead, but by the end of the first half Carlisle was ahead on Thorpe's three field goals of 23, 43, and 37 yards. In those years the dropkick was used, not the placekick of today where the ball is spotted by a ball holder. In the dropkick the kicker stood alone, as a punter does. When the ball was snapped to him, he dropped it with one end pointing to the ground so that the ball would bounce straight up. As it bounced up, he kicked it.

In the second half Harvard rallied for a 15–9 lead, but then Thorpe took over. Carrying the ball on nine consecutive plays, he slammed across the goal line for a touchdown and dropkicked the extra point, creating a 15–15 tie; touchdowns were worth 5 points then. In the final minutes Carlisle moved to the Crimson's 43-yard line. On fourth down, standing at the 50-yard line, Thorpe lined up for a field-goal attempt. His dropkick sailed between the uprights. Carlisle won, 18–15, with Thorpe having scored all his

Jim Thorpe, displaying one of football's forgotten arts—the drop kick.

team's points. Harvard would not lose another game until 1915, and in his locker room Haughton marveled at Thorpe's performance.

"Watching him turn the ends, slash off tackle, kick, and tackle," the Harvard coach said, "I realized that there was the theoretical super player in flesh and blood."

The next year Thorpe won his Olympic gold medals, which later were taken away from him when it was disclosed in 1913 that he had received about sixty dollars a month to play semipro baseball in North Carolina in 1908 and 1909, a common practice among collegians of that era. He had played under his real name instead of adopting a fictitious name, as most other players did. Rule 26 of the Olympic charter forbade an athlete from competing in the Games if he or she had been paid to play a sport—even if it were different from his or her Olympic sport.

"I was not very wise in the ways of the world," Thorpe wrote in a letter of apology to the Amateur Athletic Union, "and did not realize this was wrong."

Thorpe died in 1953, still bitter over having his Olympic medals taken away. "I won them, didn't I?" he said in 1948. "Why don't they give them back to me? They're no good to anyone else, are they?" Finally, in 1981, after decades of campaigning by Thorpe's family, the International Olympic Committee finally restored Thorpe's amateur status and agreed to replace his medals and trophies.

During the 1984 Olympic Games in Los Angeles, his medals and trophies were on display, a reminder of what he had accomplished in 1912.

After the 1912 Olympics, Thorpe returned to Carlisle and resumed playing football. With his field goals and extra points, he accounted for 198 points that season, including 25 touchdowns. The next year he joined baseball's New York Giants as an outfielder. Never a regular, he was later traded to the Cincinnati Reds, back to the Giants, and then to the Boston Braves. He had his best season in 1919, batting .327.

During the years Thorpe was playing major league baseball in the summer, he also played football in the fall for the Canton (Ohio) Bulldogs, one of the early professional teams.

In 1915 Thorpe kicked field goals of 45 and 18 yards in a 6–0 victory for the Bulldogs over the rival Massillon (Ohio) Tigers—described in the *Cleveland Plain Dealer* as "the two greatest aggregations of ex–college football stars ever gathered on professional teams in Ohio." That was the same game in which Thorpe opposed Knute Rockne, who occasionally played for the Tigers while he was an assistant coach at Notre Dame.

That was one of Rockne's last games as a player. After having been Jesse Harper's assistant coach for four seasons, he took command as Notre Dame's coach in 1918—only five years after he had helped put Notre Dame on the football map and the forward pass into football vocabulary in a startling upset of Army.

Knute (pronounced Nōōt) Kenneth Rockne had been born on March 4, 1888, in Voss, Norway, where his father Lars manufactured carriages. The carriages were so beautiful that one earned a prize at the Great Liverpool Fair in England. When his father read about the Chicago World's Fair in 1891, he built another carriage, hoping to win a prize there, too. When that carriage won the grand prize in Chicago, his father decided to remain in that growing midwestern city. He wrote to his wife Martha and asked her to come to Chicago with their three children.

Knute was five years old when he saw the Statue of Liberty from the deck of a boat steaming up the New York bay. Later, as a Chicago schoolboy, Rockne washed windows and delivered packages for pocket money. But his heart was in sports, primarily track-and-field—so much so that his father suggested that college was beyond him, that he should drop out of high school and get a job. He worked in the Chicago post office while he trained at the Illinois Athletic Club as a half-miler and pole-vaulter. But he wanted to pursue his ambition to be a college athlete. He applied

ROCKNE.

Knute Rockne as an
end at Notre Dame
was only 5-9 and
155 pounds.

to Notre Dame, then a small college, which allowed him to take an entrance exam even though he did not have a high school diploma. He passed. As a freshman, Rockne was twenty-two years old, but older college students were not unusual in those years.

By chance Rockne's roommate was Charles (Gus) Dorais, of Chippewa Falls, Wisconsin, where he had been a high school football star. Three years later their names would be carved into football history.

Rockne had not played much football as a Chicago schoolboy. But at Notre Dame he quickly developed into a dependable end, even though he was only 5–9 and 155 pounds, somewhat small even then. As the team's captain-elect in 1913, he was about to leave the campus for his summer vacation when Coach Jesse Harper mentioned that a game had been scheduled with Army at West Point, New York, on November 1, the first time that Notre Dame would play one of the established eastern teams. Rockne and Dorais later visited Harper in his office.

"Can we take a couple of footballs with us?" Rockne asked. "We've got summer jobs together at a resort on Lake Erie, and we want to do some special practicing."

Harper tossed them two footballs. But what even the coach didn't realize at the time was that Rockne and Dorais were hoping to take advantage of some new rules governing the forward pass. First allowed in 1906, the forward pass had been used by some teams, although not extensively. But in their private workouts during off-hours from their jobs as waiters, Dorais polished his skill at throwing a football with a perfect spiral (even though it was a much fatter, rounder ball), and Rockne learned to catch a pass in full stride.

"Mobility and change of pace," Rockne kept telling Dorais. "They're not going to know where we're going or when we get there."

On returning to the Notre Dame campus, they put on a display of passing and catching that convinced Harper of its usefulness. Wisely the coach did not use much passing in three one-sided victories—87–0 over Ohio Northern, 20–7 over North Dakota, and 62–0 over Alma, a small Michigan school. Harper was saving the surprise for Army, which was stunned in a 35–13 upset.

Army had led at halftime, 14–13, but then Dorais and Rockne took over. In the second half, Dorais completed 10 of 13 passes, with Rockne catching 7. For the game Dorais completed 14 of 17 for 243 yards.

On the sports pages of *The New York Times* the next day, a headline read: NOTRE DAME OPEN PLAY AMAZES ARMY. The story praised the "most sensational football ever seen in the East," a tribute to what Rockne and Dorais had devised. The introduction of the forward pass as an offensive weapon would be only the beginning of Rockne's contributions to football. As the Notre Dame coach for thirteen seasons through 1930, he would produce a record of 105 victories against only 12 losses and 5 ties for a remarkable .897 percentage. He would have five unbeaten seasons (1919, 1920, 1924, 1929, and 1930). He would have two teams recognized as national champions (1924 and 1930).

The 1924 team would inspire one of football's most famous nicknames—the Four Horsemen.

Notre Dame defeated Army, 12–7, at the Polo Grounds in New York City that year, shortly after the release of the motion picture *The Four Horsemen of the Apocalypse,* starring Rudolf Valentino,

one of Hollywood's most popular stars. In the press box after the game, Grantland Rice, then one of America's leading sportswriters and a columnist for the *New York Tribune,* began typing.

"Outlined against a blue-gray October sky," he wrote, "the Four Horsemen rode again. In dramatic lore they were known as Famine, Pestilence, Destruction, and Death. These are only aliases. Their real names are Stuhldreher, Miller, Crowley, and Layden . . ."

The Four Horsemen: Miller, Layden, Crowley, Stuhldreher.

When the team assembled for practice on Monday in South Bend, four horses and a photographer were waiting. George Strickler, later a sports columnist for the *Chicago Tribune* and then Notre Dame's sports information director, posed Harry Stuhldreher, Don Miller, Jim Crowley, and Elmer Layden on horseback, each wearing his helmet and holding a football. That photo established the Four Horsemen as the most celebrated backfield in football history, then or now.

Four years later Rockne's 1928 team would justify one of football's most famous phrases: "Win one for the Gipper."

George Gipp had been a gifted halfback in 1920, a triple threat as a runner, passer, and punter. On defense he was a sure tackler. He also had a sense of self-confidence that Rockne quickly understood.

"I learned very early," Rockne once said, "to place full confidence in his self-confidence."

For all of Gipp's self-confidence, he was somewhat of a loner. He wasn't interested in publicity. He seldom granted interviews or posed for photos. For that 1920 season Gipp not only was named by Walter Camp to the All-America team, but he also was selected as the nation's outstanding college player. Had there been a Heisman Trophy that year, Gipp probably would have won it. But when Notre Dame completed its season with a 25–0 victory over Michigan State, he was in the college infirmary at South Bend with a life-threatening infection. Antibiotic drugs had not yet been developed. Gipp's condition quickly worsened. Soon he had pneumonia.

"Someday in a tough game," he told Rockne, a daily visitor to his bedside, "ask the players to win one for the Gipper."

In 1928, before a game with Army at Yankee Stadium, the

coach walked to the center of the locker room to address his team. His players had been in grammar school when Gipp had died, but each knew of his fame. Rockne told them about what Gipp had said on his deathbed.

"I've never used that request until now," Rockne said. "But this is the time."

Notre Dame won that game, 12–6, on a touchdown pass from Butch Niemiec to Johnny O'Brien in the closing minutes. The legend of George Gipp would drift through the decades to come. In the motion picture *Rockne*, the role of the halfback was played by Ronald Reagan, who later became the President of the United States; Rockne was portrayed by Pat O'Brien.

On March 31, 1931, at the peak of his fame, the forty-three-year-old Notre Dame coach was aboard Transcontinental Western Flight 955 out of Kansas City, bound for Los Angeles, where he was to sign a motion picture contract. Suddenly in the skies over the Kansas farmland, the plane sputtered, then it crashed. Knute was dead. But what he accomplished at Notre Dame, both as a player and as a coach, helped guide football into its present role in American society.

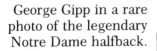

George Gipp in a rare photo of the legendary Notre Dame halfback.

1930-1945

George Halas and the T-Formation

One day during Calvin Coolidge's administration, an Illinois senator introduced George Halas and Red Grange to the President.

"These gentlemen," the senator explained, "are with the Chicago Bears."

"How interesting," the President said, "I've always enjoyed animal acts."

At the time not everybody, certainly not President Coolidge, was aware of pro football. But more than any other two people in the evolution of the game, George Halas and Red Grange taught America that when a football player left college, his career was merely beginning. One of pro football's Hall of Fame coaches, Weeb Ewbank, often joked that "hindsight is twenty-twenty," meaning that it's easy to look back and be correct. In looking back at National Football League history, it's easy to realize that 1933 was its turning point.

Until then the NFL had been a hodgepodge. In its maiden season, 1921, teams represented six cities that currently have franchises (Chicago, Green Bay, Cleveland, Cincinnati, Detroit, and Buffalo) as well as several smaller cities—Canton, Akron, Dayton, Columbus, Rock Island, and Rochester.

Most games were played on dirt fields with small, rickety wooden grandstands. A few thousand people, sometimes only a few hundred, attended. In its early years the NFL not only was without many spectators, but it was also without a balanced schedule or a championship game. In 1926, for example, the NFL had twenty-two teams, with the Frankford (Pennsylvania) Yellowjackets having a 14–1–1 record for first place while the Hammond (Indiana) Pros and the Louisville (Kentucky) Colonels shared last place, each with a 0–4 record.

Year by year after that, the NFL slowly dwindled to only eight teams in 1932. But for the 1933 season the NFL was split into Eastern and Western divisions, each with five teams. When the winners of the two divisions met in the first NFL championship game, the Bears defeated the New York Giants, 23–21, on a razzle-dazzle last-second 32-yard touchdown—a fake smash into the line by fullback Bronko Nagurski, who stopped and threw a pass to end Bill Hewitt, who then lateraled to end Bill Karr for the touchdown.

Competitively that first NFL championship game was the equivalent of today's Super Bowl game. But financially the players' share reflected the Depression that had so many Americans out of work. The bonus check for each member of the Bears was $210.23.

Red Grange received one of those checks. The halfback was in his next-to-last season with the Bears by then, but in 1925 he had become pro football's first national attraction. As an All-American at Illinois, he was known as "the Galloping Ghost," a single-wing tailback best remembered for his performance against Michigan in the 1924 dedication of the Illinois stadium. He returned the

In 1933 NFL championship game, end Bill Hewitt laterals to end Bill Karr.

opening kickoff 95 yards for a touchdown, returned a punt 67 yards for a touchdown, then scored on runs of 54 yards and 44 yards—all in the game's first twelve minutes.

Grange later scored on a 13-yard run and threw a 20-yard touchdown pass. Before the game ended in a 39–14 victory, he had run for 212 yards in 15 carries, completed 6 passes for 64 yards, scored 5 touchdowns, and passed for another.

But the Michigan student newspaper minimized Grange's performance, declaring, "All Grange can do is run." That prompted Bob Zuppke, the Illinois coach, to compare Grange to a famous opera singer of that era, saying, "And all Galli-Curci can do is sing." Immediately after Grange's senior season, he joined the Bears for a barnstorming tour arranged by C. C. (Cash and Carry) Pyle, a fast-talking promoter. Grange earned a quick $100,000, a stupendous sum at the time. But his decision had been opposed even by Zuppke, who typified the disdain that college coaches had for pro football then.

"Football," the Illinois coach told him, "just isn't a game to be played for money."

"You get paid for coaching, Zup," Grange retorted. "Why is it wrong for me to get paid for playing?"

Grange was paid handsomely. But he earned every cent, as did his Bear teammates. Beginning with the first sellout crowd ever for a pro football game, 36,000 at Wrigley Field on Thanksgiving Day 1925 through January 31, 1926, Grange and the Bears played nineteen games before a total of nearly four hundred thousand spectators in seventeen cities as they criss-crossed the country. At the Polo Grounds in New York, he attracted at least 65,000, plus uncounted thousands who scaled the bleacher walls. At the Los Angeles Coliseum he drew more than 75,000.

"No one," a weary Grange said afterward, "will ever attempt anything like this again."

No one ever has. But with that tour Grange established himself in the era known as the Roaring Twenties as *the* football player. He was to football then what Babe Ruth was to baseball, Jack Dempsey to boxing, Bobby Jones to golf, Bill Tilden to tennis. But the NFL wasn't yet strong enough to absorb him. Grange and Pyle demanded one-third ownership in the Bears, but Halas and his partner, Dutch Sternaman, refused.

Red Grange breaking away as an All-America halfback at Illinois.

Seeking their own stage, Grange and Pyle formed the American Football League for the 1926 season. Grange was the co-owner and halfback of the New York Yankees in this new league. When the AFL folded after one season, the Yankees joined the NFL for the 1927 season. Grange missed most of that season because of a damaged knee, the most prevalent injury in football—then or now. This is especially true for a running back whose legs are hit when he is tackled. To prevent this injury, some players now wear light metal-and-rubber knee braces that absorb the shock of contact. Red Grange never had the opportunity to wear a protective knee brace, but in 1929 he rejoined the Bears, his disagreement with Halas forgotten.

Halas, who died in 1983 at age eighty-eight, was one of the founders of the NFL on September 17, 1920, at a meeting in Canton, Ohio.

Men from twelve midwestern cities gathered that day in Ralph Hay's showroom for the Hupmobile, a popular automobile at the time. Halas was there representing the Decatur (Illinois) Staleys, who would move to Chicago in 1921 and one year later be nicknamed the Bears.

"We only had two chairs at that meeting," Halas often recalled. "Everybody else sat on the runningboards or the fenders."

In the beginning Halas was a rare triple threat—owner, coach, and captain (as right end on offense and defense). By the time he stopped coaching at age seventy-three, his record (including playoff games) over four separate ten-year tenures was 325–151–31 (.673) and the Bears had won eight NFL titles. Only the Green Bay Packers had won more: eleven. But the tough, crusty man known as the Papa Bear always argued that his team

George Halas, the Papa Bear, questioning a call: "I'm sure I was right."

also should have been declared the 1924 champion despite the Cleveland Bulldogs' better record. In those years, before there was a championship game between the two division winners, the NFL title was awarded at a league meeting.

"I left the meeting to go to the washroom," Halas said. "And when I got back, they had voted the championship to Cleveland."

Halas had the personality of the pioneer he was. At the Pro Football Hall of Fame in Canton, Ohio, he once stared at a photo in which he was shown arguing with a referee.

"I don't know what I was talking about," he said, "but I'm sure I was right."

He usually was right. He was sixty-eight when he coached the Bears to the NFL title in 1963, defeating the Giants at Wrigley Field, 14–10.

"There isn't room," he said the next day, "for many of these things in one lifetime."

In his lifetime the Papa Bear had more room than most people. In addition to his championship teams, he virtually created a private wing for the Bears at the Pro Football Hall of Fame shrine. In addition to Halas himself, nineteen members were established Bear players during their careers, more than that of any other team—Doug Atkins, George Blanda, Dick Butkus, George Connor, Paddy Driscoll, Danny Fortmann, Bill George, Red Grange, Ed Healy, Bill Hewitt, Sid Luckman, Link Lyman, George McAfee, George Musso, Bronko Nagurski, Gale Sayers, Joe Stydahar, George Trafton, and Bulldog Turner.

"Nagurski," the Papa Bear once said of his fullback of the thirties, "what a man!"

Nagurski, at 6-2 and 225 pounds, had joined the Bears from the

University of Minnesota, where he actually had been chosen for two positions on one 1929 All-America team—fullback and tackle. In those years All-America teams consisted of only eleven positions, since a player had to perform on both offense and defense. Nagurski's strength was legendary. His Minnesota coach, Fats Spears, often joked that he found Bronko plowing a field near his hometown of International Falls, Minnesota.

"I stopped to ask directions," Spears would say, "but instead of pointing with his hand, Bronko pointed with the plow."

Nagurski enjoyed going along with that gag. Soon after he joined the Bears, some older players teased him about his strength. One player asked him how he got so strong.

"Plowing fields," he said.

"That's nothing," one of the Bears said. "Most of us have plowed a field at one time or another."

"Without a horse?" Bronko said.

But on the football field nobody joked about Nagurski's strength. In a game at Wrigley Field, he smashed through several tacklers on a 35-yard touchdown run and careened into the end zone. Unable to stop in time, he crashed into the brick wall beyond. Old-timers insist that the ivy on that wall covers a crack that Nagurski put in the bricks.

"I don't know if I cracked the wall," he said years later. "I have a feeling it was cracked before. But I did hit it pretty hard."

His famous teammate, Red Grange, often insisted that he was fortunate to have played with Nagurski rather than against him.

"I had to try to tackle Bronk in scrimmages occasionally," Grange once recalled, "and there was something strange about tackling him. When you hit him, it was almost like getting an electric shock."

Bronko Nagurski was named to the 1929 All-America team at two positions.

Opposing players knew the feeling. On a road trip the train carrying the Pittsburgh team had to slam to a sudden stop, spilling the players out of their seats. One of the Steelers shook his head.

"We've hit Nagurski," he joked.

For eight seasons Nagurski terrorized NFL tacklers as the Bears' fullback before he joined the wrestling circuit. But in 1943, with the NFL's manpower depleted by World War II, he rejoined the Bears at age thirty-five after a lapse of six years. Used at tackle for most of the season, he returned to fullback for the Bears' last two games. In wrapping up the Western Division title against the rival Chicago Cardinals, he gained 81 yards in 15 car-

Bronko Nagurski of the Bears crashing into two Giants in 1934 title game.

ries. In the NFL title game, he scored the touchdown that provided the Bears with a lead they never relinquished.

"Bronko wasn't a spectacular breakaway runner," Halas once said, "but for football purists he was a picture runner. He had perfect form for a fullback. He ran so low to the ground that his back was almost parallel to it. And at the moment of contact with a tackler, he dipped his shoulder and brought it up with terrific impact, like an uppercut. It made no difference how much momentum the tackler had or how much he weighed. Bronko's countersmash with his shoulder bounced the tackler off him like rain hitting a tin roof."

Bronko Nagurski had been the symbol of the Bears' power as a running team. Then, in 1934, the NFL changed the shape of the ball slightly. Longer and narrower, it made passing easier. And in 1939 a rookie quarterback named Sid Luckman joined the Bears and soon turned it into the NFL's most feared passing team.

At the time, the modern T-formation was considered to be a

radical offense. Clark Shaughnessy, the Stanford coach, designed it with the backs in the form of a T—the quarterback crouched behind the center, the fullback lined up directly behind the quarterback, the two halfbacks on each side of the fullback. Shaughnessy had developed it at the University of Chicago as Amos Alonzo Stagg's successor. But at Stanford, which had won only one game in 1939, he used the T-formation to turn the 1940 team into the Rose Bowl champion with a 10–0 record. His stars were left-handed quarterback Frankie Albert, halfbacks Hugh Gallarneau and Pete Kmetovic, and fullback Norm Standlee.

"A lesser coach," Albert said, "would have been afraid to try something so radical. We were skeptical, but he sold us on it."

Some of the Bear players probably were skeptical, too. But with Luckman at quarterback the Bears dazzled the NFL with the T-formation that turned the single-wing offense into a dinosaur.

"Luckman could do it all," Halas once said. "Pass, run, kick, defend, and think."

While at Columbia University, the 6-0, 200-pound Luckman had known only the single-wing offense, which was geared to the tailback running or passing on almost every play. When he reported to the Bears, he suddenly had to learn the new and complicated T-formation. Halas assigned one of his assistant coaches, Luke Johnsos, to tutor the rookie passer. In his first year Luckman was the backup quarterback. Halas wanted it that way. The Bears' playbook had 350 plays, many with several variations. Halas knew that Luckman needed time to memorize and master all those plays.

By the 1940 season Luckman was in command. So were the Bears, who won the Western Division title with an 8–3 record, qualifying for the NFL championship game against the Redskins in Washington that would provide the most famous score in NFL history.

When the Bears arrived in the nation's capital, they read in the Washington newspaper that some of the Redskins had called them "crybabies," a reference to the Redskins' 7–3 victory over the Bears earlier that season. In the locker room before the game, George Halas didn't give a pep talk. He didn't even raise his voice. He simply held up the newspapers and pointed to red-crayon circles around the Redskin quotes.

"Gentlemen," the coach said, "we're not crybabies. Go out and play the football you can."

With a roar, the Bears burst onto the field. Moments later, on

One of the NFL's best passers, Sid Luckman of the Bears could also run.

their first play from scrimmage, they had a touchdown—a 68-yard run around left end by fullback Bill Osmanski behind perfect blocking. The next time the Bears got the ball, an 80-yard march ended with Luckman sneaking across the goal line. Not long after that, Joe Maniaci dashed 42 yards for another touchdown. By halftime the Bears led 28–0, and they rolled to a crushing 73–0 victory. The score established that the Bears were a special team, that Sid Luckman was a special quarterback, and that the T-formation was a special offense.

The Bears won the NFL title again in 1941, 1943, and 1946—all with Luckman at quarterback.

But to some of his teammates, Luckman's finest moment occurred when the Bears, as the 1943 champions, were playing the College All-Stars at the start of the 1944 exhibition season. When the All-Stars jumped to a 14–0 lead, Luckman began growling in the huddle.

"Where did you men get those uniforms—steal them?" he snapped. "Those uniforms are not supposed to be disgraced."

Responding to the challenge, the Bears won, 24–21. In their locker room later, center Bulldog Turner and guard George Musso, each of whom would be inducted later into the Pro Football Hall of Fame, looked over at their quarterback.

"Sid, you're the greatest," Turner said. "You picked all of us up by our cleats and made us win this game."

"Nobody else could have done it," Musso said. "I've seen you do some great things, but this was the greatest."

In those years, the Washington Redskins also had a special passer—Slingin' Sammy Baugh, a whipcord Texan with an arm like a lariat. When he took off his burgundy-and-gold Redskin jer-

When his career ended, Sammy Baugh held 16 NFL passing records.

sey for the last time after sixteen seasons, he held sixteen NFL passing records and three NFL punting records. Out of Texas Christian University, he had been special from the day he reported to the Redskins' training camp as a rookie. Coach Ray Flaherty was diagraming the team's pass plays on a blackboard.

"On this one," Flaherty said, "I want you to hit the receiver in the eye."

Baugh looked up at his new coach. "One question," he said, "which eye?"

When the Redskins were demolished by the Bears in that 1940 NFL championship game, Sammy Baugh didn't have any excuses. Many of the Redskin rooters in Griffith Stadium that day believed it might have been a different game if end Charley Malone had not missed a touchdown pass when the Bears had an early 7–0 lead. Malone lost Baugh's pass in the sun, the ball hitting him in the chest and falling to the ground.

"Suppose Malone had caught that ball," Baugh was asked later, "would that have changed the game?"

"It might have," Baugh said, forcing a smile for the reporters. "It might have made it 73–7."

Two years later Baugh and the Redskins would upset the Bears in the NFL championship game, 14–6. But over a span of fourteen seasons starting in 1933, the Bears won five NFL championships and eight Western Division titles—far more than any other team of that era.

By then, nobody confused George Halas or the Bears with an animal act.

1945-1960

The Black Knights and Johnny U

In the years after World War II, the Army team was known as the "Black Knights of the Hudson"—"Black Knights" because they wore black jerseys with gold numbers and gold helmets, "of the Hudson" because they represented the United States Military Academy, which is situated on the craggy cliffs of West Point above the Hudson River.

Of all those Black Knights, two remain on a pedestal today— Felix (Doc) Blanchard and Glenn Davis. Blanchard was a fullback, Davis a halfback. Their nicknames were "Mister Inside" and "Mister Outside." Blanchard won the Heisman Trophy as the nation's outstanding college player in 1945; Davis won it the next year. During their three seasons together, they scored a total of 89 touchdowns (51 by Davis, 38 by Blanchard). In that time Army never lost a game, winning 27 and tying 1 (a memorable 0–0 struggle with Notre Dame in 1946).

"Blanchard and Davis were the best one-two punch, in my belief," their coach, Colonel Earl (Red) Blaik, later wrote, "that college football ever saw."

Other college teams have had a single player who arguably was better than either Blanchard or Davis, but few college teams have

44

"Mr. Inside," fullback Doc Blanchard, avoids Michigan tacklers in 1945.

ever had two players at their level at the same time. In the history of the Heisman Trophy, first awarded in 1935, they were the only two running backs from the same college to win it in consecutive years. Decades later their time at Army is still remembered as the Blanchard-Davis era.

Blanchard was not only husky and strong at 6-1 and 208 pounds, but he was also fast. He could toss the 16-pound shot put 52 feet and run the 100-yard dash in 10 seconds flat. In addition to his battering-ram style as a fullback, he was an agile pass catcher, a devastating blocker, and a bruising linebacker on defense. He also could punt and kick off. He was a complete player.

"Blanchard is as good as Nagurski," said Steve Owen, then the New York Giants' coach, "only he has more finesse."

"Blanchard," said Herman Hickman, then Army's offensive line coach, "is the only man who runs his own interference."

As a blocker Blanchard also ran interference for Davis, a swift breakaway threat who one season averaged a remarkable 11.7 yards each time he carried the ball. He also was a good passer and a good pass receiver. As a defensive back he was a sure tackler. Much of his talent was geared to sheer speed. He ran the 100-yard dash in less than 10 seconds.

"Glenn Davis was emphatically the fastest halfback I ever knew," Colonel Blaik once said. "He was not so much a dodger and sidestepper as a blazing runner who had a fourth and even a fifth gear in reserve, could change direction at top speed and fly away from tacklers as if jet-propelled."

Whenever Colonel Blaik reminisced about Davis, the coach enjoyed remembering a 20–13 victory over Michigan when the Army quarterback, Arnold Tucker, was unable to lift his right

"Mr. Outside," halfback Glenn Davis, stiff-arms a tackler in 1943.

arm because of an injury. Lacking his best passer, the Cadets' coach designed a game plan in which Davis would do the passing, often on option plays.

"He completed 7 out of 8 for 168 yards, accounting for our first touchdown and setting up the third," Colonel Blaik said. "He also ran through guard for 59 yards and our second touchdown."

Davis was somewhat small at 5-9, but he was a sturdy 170 pounds. He would go on to play for the Los Angeles Rams, helping them win the 1951 NFL title after serving as an Army lieutenant. Blanchard never played in the NFL, preferring to stay in the Army Air Force as a pilot. While based in England in 1959, he survived a crash landing. He had stayed with his jet fighter rather than parachute and let it fall into a London residential area.

But in Army history Blanchard is remembered best for his exploits as a football player.

"For a big man," Colonel Blaik once recalled, "he was the quickest starter I ever saw. In the open he ran with the niftiness as well as the speed of a great halfback. Twice in Navy games, I saw him run through a head-on tackle without breaking stride and race on to a touchdown."

One time, though, Blanchard did not run through a tackle. It was during the Army-Notre Dame rivalry.

During the first two years of the Blanchard-Davis era, Army often was accused of dominating other college teams that had lost some of their best players to military service during World War II. But by 1946 the colleges had regained many of those players. Notre Dame in particular was a powerhouse again after 59–0 and 48–0 losses to Army the previous two years. Their rivalry resumed at Yankee Stadium.

"When two great teams meet," Frank Leahy, the Notre Dame coach, said later, "defense tends to dominate."

Their famous 0–0 tie was preserved by defense, if not by one tackle. From the Army 42-yard line, Blanchard thundered around right end and appeared on his way to a touchdown. But from across the field, Johnny Lujack, who is best remembered as the Notre Dame quarterback but was also a defensive back, angled toward the big fullback. With a low tackle Lujack tumbled Blanchard at the Notre Dame 36-yard line.

Army would go on to remain undefeated in 32 consecutive games before losing to Columbia, 21–20, in 1947, an upset sparked by end Bill Swiacki's spectacular catches. But the Blanchard-Lujack collision will always be considered the most memorable moment of that time, the moment that symbolized the transition from the Blanchard-Davis era to the Frank Leahy era.

A Notre Dame tackle during Knute Rockne's reign, Leahy returned there in 1941 as the new head coach. Including two earlier seasons at Boston College, Leahy's career record at the time of his 1953 retirement due to illness was 107–13–9. He had six unbeaten Notre Dame teams, including four recognized as national champions. Each of those four championship teams had a Heisman Trophy winner—quarterback Angelo Bertelli in 1943 (using T-formation plays borrowed from the Chicago Bears), quarterback Johnny Lujack in 1947, end Leon Hart in 1949, and halfback Johnny Lattner in 1953. Usually a pessimist, Leahy spoke with a scholarly vocabulary that mesmerized his players.

"At times a defeat is an asset," he once said. "It may have countless other effects that will outweigh the disadvantages concomitant with defeat."

Even so, Leahy's teams were seldom defeated. During his devotion to Notre Dame's tradition, he once was approached by Mickey McBride, the co-owner of the Cleveland franchise in the All-America Football Conference that planned to start operations in 1946 as the NFL's rival. McBride wanted to hire Leahy as the Cleveland coach, but Leahy declined.

"If you think I am a worthy coach," he told McBride, "then you will be pleased by Paul Brown—we are one and the same in our philosophies toward the game."

In a sense Paul Brown was the product of another tradition—the continuing popularity of the game in Massillon, Ohio—first during pro football's early years and later with the Massillon High School team, which Brown coached to an 80–8–2 record over nine seasons. He moved on to Ohio State and, during World War II, to the Great Lakes Naval Station team, which was based near Chicago and had some of the nation's best college players. He was still there when Leahy recommended him as the coach of the Cleveland team in the AAFC.

Brown not only was hired, but the team also was named after him—the Cleveland Browns.

Brown was such a good coach, he created a monster of a team that was so efficient it destroyed the element of competition in the AAFC and, following the 1949 season, the league itself. In four seasons the Browns won four championships while accumulating a regular-season record of 47–4–3. Before the 1950 season the NFL absorbed three AAFC teams—the Browns, the San Francisco 49ers, and the Baltimore Colts. But the NFL establishment snickered at the thought that the Browns might be as good as the best NFL teams, especially the 1949 champion Philadelphia Eagles.

"To me," said Earle (Greasy) Neale, the coach of the Eagles, "the Browns are a basketball team. All they can do is throw."

True, the Browns had dominated the AAFC with Otto Graham throwing passes to his ends, Dante Lavelli and Mac Speedie, and to Dub Jones, a halfback who often lined up far to the right as one of the first flankerbacks. But the Browns did more than throw. With the 238-pound Marion Motley at fullback, they ran. And if their offense sputtered, they salvaged field goals with Lou (The Toe) Groza as their placekicker. They also had a dependable defensive unit, with Bill Willis at middle guard.

Paul Brown, whose Cleveland teams won 10 consecutive divisional titles.

Quietly, around the same time that Jackie Robinson was breaking in as the first black player in major league baseball, Paul Brown had helped to integrate pro football with Motley and Willis in 1946.

During the early years of pro football, several black players had

Marion Motley, one of the first black NFL players, slams past a tackler.

been on the small-town teams of the period. Fritz Pollard, an All-America running back at Brown University, not only played on some of those early teams but also coached. Paul Robeson, an All-America end at Rutgers, played at Akron and Milwaukee before deciding to concentrate on a singing career. But in the growth of the NFL, black players had mostly been ignored until the Los Angeles Rams signed Kenny Washington and Woody Strode in 1946.

George Taliferro, a running back from Indiana selected by the Bears in 1949, was the first black college player chosen in the NFL draft. But he decided to sign with the Los Angeles Dons of the AAFC.

By then Motley and Willis were recognized as two of the Browns' best players. Perhaps with the idea of deflating the team in its NFL debut in 1950, the Browns were scheduled to open their season in Philadelphia against the defending champion Eagles, but the plan backfired. The Browns won, 35–10, as Graham threw 3 touchdown passes and scored another touchdown himself. He completed 21 of 38 passes for 346 yards as the Browns accumulated 487 yards of total offense. After the game, Pete Pihos, an Eagle pass receiver on two NFL championship teams, was asked by his wife what had happened.

"Honey," he said, "we met a team from the big league."

Paul Brown had molded a team that would win the NFL's Eastern Division title every season from 1950 through 1955 as well as three NFL championships in that span. More than that, Brown would popularize the organizational approach not only to pro football but also to college football.

Many of the techniques that are accepted procedure now were

unknown until Brown introduced them—year-round coaching staffs, notebooks and classrooms, film scouting, grading players from film study, lodging the team at a hotel the night before home games, specific pass patterns, face bars on helmets, switching offensive players to defense, using messenger guards to bring in the next play from the sideline. He also exercised complete control over the Browns' organization.

"Complete control," he once said. "There is no other way for a team to operate and be a winner."

Wearing sneakers on a frozen field, Otto Graham freezes a tackler.

That complete control was eroded after Art Modell, a New York advertising executive, purchased the Browns in 1961. Following the 1962 season, Paul Brown was out, only to surface six years later as part-owner and coach of the Cincinnati Bengals, a team that eventually qualified for Super Bowl XVI as the 1981 American Conference champions, with Forrest Gregg as coach.

Meanwhile, one of Paul Brown's disciples, Wilbur (Weeb) Ewbank, developed the Baltimore Colts into a two-time NFL champion, the 23–17 winner of what is often called "the greatest game ever played"—the 1958 NFL championship game with the New York Giants that required the first sudden-death overtime in NFL history.

After having been Paul Brown's offensive line coach, Ewbank took command of the Colts in 1954 with a five-year plan. According to his timetable, the Colts would be a title contender in 1958. As it turned out, they won the NFL championship that year. But in addition to Ewbank's coaching and the talent of many skilled players, the Colts had discovered a Hall of Fame quarterback, Johnny Unitas, for the price of what in 1956 was an eighty-five-cent long-distance phone call from Baltimore to Pittsburgh.

Unitas had had an inconspicuous career as a college quarterback at the University of Louisville. Then he had been released as a rookie by the Pittsburgh Steelers during training camp in 1955. He returned to the city of Pittsburgh, where he had grown up. He got a construction job working on a pile driver and played semipro football with the Bloomfield Rams of the Greater Pittsburgh League for six dollars a game.

"We played Wednesdays and Saturday nights," he once recalled. "We sort of made up the plays as we went along. I'd tell

Johnny Unitas, from $6 a game to two NFL titles with the Baltimore Colts.

the receivers what patterns to run, and I'd pass to the one who looked most open. Each team only had about three or four good players, and they could do pretty much what they wanted against the rest. At the same time you might have a 140-pound blocker trying to hold off a 225-pound lineman crashing in on you, so you had to take punishment. I was hardened enough to escape injury. We won the league championship, which was more satisfying than the six dollars a game I was getting. It was football, and I was able to keep in practice."

Unitas was hoping that the Browns, who had corresponded with him, might invite him to their 1956 training camp.

"No need for you this season," Paul Brown had told Unitas in a telegram after the Steelers had cut him. "Suggest you come to camp next summer for tryout. Contact me in the spring."

But one day in February 1956, Don Kellett, the Colts' general manager, phoned Unitas at his Pittsburgh home.

"We'd like to get a look at you," Kellett said. "We have a tryout camp in May. Why don't you come down and work out?"

Unitas made the Colts as a second-stringer. In their fourth game that season, with the Colts leading the Bears, 21–20, their starting quarterback, George Shaw, suffered a serious knee injury. Unitas was inserted. But his inexperience was obvious. He fumbled three times and had another pass intercepted as the Colts lost, 58–27. Another coach might have been impatient with the rookie, but Ewbank consoled him.

"Don't worry about it," the coach said. "You're my quarterback again next week."

By the end of that 1956 season, Johnny U, as he came to be known, had established himself. By the end of the 1957 season, he was voted the second-team All-Pro quarterback behind Y. A. Tittle of the San Francisco 49ers, a ten-year veteran. By the end of the 1958 season, he was looked upon as the NFL's best quarterback, especially after his performance in the championship

Johnny U, one of the last NFL players to wear high-topped football shoes.

game that season—the one he put into sudden-death overtime.

In the dusk at Yankee Stadium, the scoreboard clock blinked 1:56—one minute and fifty-six seconds to play. Not much time. Perhaps not enough time for the Colts, who were losing, 17–14.

After having forced the Giants to punt, the Colts had the ball on their own 14-yard line. But they had to get close enough to kick a tying field goal in order to force sudden-death overtime. As the Colt offense trotted onto the field, Unitas hunched into the huddle.

"Unless the clock is stopped," he said, "we won't have time for any more huddles. Stay alert. I'll call the plays at the line of scrimmage."

Unitas threw a pass to halfback Lenny Moore for an 11-yard gain; then he completed another pass to wide receiver Raymond Berry, a 25-yard gain to midfield. Quickly he hit Berry again at the Giants' 35-yard line, then found him at the 13-yard line. With the clock flashing the final seconds, Steve Myhra, the Colts' place-kicker, hurried onto the field. Quickly he booted a 20-yard field goal with seven seconds remaining to tie the score at 17–17.

In overtime the Giants won the toss and elected to receive the kickoff. But the Colt defense forced a punt.

Starting at their own 20, the Colts marched deep into Giant territory. On second down at the 8-yard line, Unitas called a daring play—a sideline pass to tight end Jim Mutscheller that, had a Giant intercepted, might have backfired into a Giant touchdown. Instead the cool crew-cut quarterback hit Mutscheller at the 1-yard line. On third down, fullback Alan Ameche blasted into the end zone. The Colts had won, 23–17.

"That pass to Mutscheller," Unitas was asked later, "weren't you risking an interception?"

Alan Ameche scoring the winning touchdown in 1958 NFL title game.

"When you know what you're doing," Unitas answered, smiling, "you don't get intercepted."

In completing 26 of 40 passes for 349 yards and 1 touchdown, Johnny U had put himself into NFL history. The following season he again led the Colts to the NFL title over the Giants in the championship game. He also set one of the NFL's most revered individual records—passing for at least 1 touchdown in 47 consecutive games, football's version of Joe DiMaggio's 56-game hitting streak in baseball. But even in losing those two championship games, the Giants, who had won the NFL title in 1956, were responsible for lifting pro football to the equal of major league baseball in the hearts of many American sports followers.

In those years the Giants had several storied players—Frank Gifford and Alex Webster at running back, Charlie Conerly at quarterback, Kyle Rote at wide receiver, Andy Robustelli at defensive end, Sam Huff at middle linebacker, Jim Patton at safety, and Pat Summerall as their placekicker.

Jim Lee Howell, a tall friendly man who had once been a Giant end, was the head coach of those teams. In his quiet way Howell preferred to give credit for the team's success to two of his assistant coaches who would soon be much more famous. Vince Lombardi was in charge of the offense, Tom Landry in charge of the defense. Both would leave the Giants for the opportunity to be a head coach—Lombardi with the Green Bay Packers in 1959, Landry with the Dallas Cowboys, which became an expansion team in 1960.

The NFL had come of age. But its success had inspired the creation of a new rival, the American Football League, which eventually would make the NFL itself bigger and better.

1960-1970

Vince Lombardi and Joe Namath

In the years when Vince Lombardi was driving the Green Bay Packers to five NFL championships in seven seasons (including victories in the first two Super Bowl games), he quickly was described as a legend. But whenever the Packers' coach heard or read that, he shook his head.

"I'm not a legend," he said once. "You have to be Halas to be a legend. George Halas is seventy-four years old, and he's done something for the game. I'm not a legend."

Lombardi is a legend now. He's also a yardstick by which all current coaches are measured, especially Packer coaches. Bart Starr, his Hall of Fame quarterback, took over as the Packer coach in 1975 but in nine seasons had only moderate success. Starr was followed in 1984 by another Lombardi disciple, Forrest Gregg, a Hall of Fame offensive tackle. Gregg's burden was the same as Starr's had been—to turn the Packers into champions again, as Lombardi had. Lombardi arrived at Green Bay in 1959, after the Packers had won only one game the previous season. Gregg had been on that team, mostly as a substitute.

"I almost quit at the end of that 1958 season," Gregg later acknowledged. "I was not about to stick around if this new guy kept

Vince Lombardi of the Packers: five NFL titles in seven seasons.

the old system. But the first day of training camp, Vince Lombardi sold me on his system.''

That first day one of the Packers' pass receivers did not run a pattern precisely. He was twenty yards downfield when Lombardi began shouting at him. And the coach continued to shout until the player had returned to the huddle for the next play. Watching the scene, Gregg realized that under Lombardi none of the Packers would be able to get by with a halfhearted effort, as that pass receiver so often had the previous season.

"The year before," Gregg recalled, "nothing had ever been said to that player by any coach, no matter how much he loafed. That sold me on Lombardi; this was the kind of coach I wanted.''

As it turned out, Lombardi was the kind of coach all the Packers wanted, at least when they look back now on their glory years as members of one of the most dominant teams in NFL history. Perhaps the finest tribute to what Lombardi accomplished for those Packers is that seven of them are in the Pro Football Hall of Fame—Starr, Gregg, fullback Jim Taylor, center Jim Ringo, middle linebacker Ray Nitschke, defensive end Willie Davis, and cornerback Herb Adderley.

Quite significantly five of those Hall of Famers (Starr, Gregg, Taylor, Ringo, and Nitschke) were on the Packers before Lombardi arrived. But under his coaching they fulfilled their potential, if not exceeded it, while contributing to five championship teams: 1961, 1962, 1965, 1966, and 1967.

Through the years the Packers have won more NFL titles, eleven, than any other team. But until Lombardi arrived, the Packers had not won a title since 1944; as one of the NFL's original "town teams," they had won the championship in 1936 and

1939, and had been awarded the title in 1929, 1930, and 1931. During that era their coach was Earl (Curly) Lambeau, one of the franchise's founders on August 11, 1919, at a meeting in the *Green Bay Press-Gazette's* dingy editorial room. At the time Lambeau, who would be the team's coach through 1949, was also working for the Indian Packing Company, which he persuaded to pay for the team's uniforms. Hence the Packers' nickname, even though that firm soon went out of business.

In their first season the Packers had a 10–1 record against teams from other Wisconsin and Michigan towns. By 1921 the Packers joined the NFL for its first season, losing to the Chicago Bears, 20–0, in the start of what would be the NFL's most enduring rivalry.

Within a decade the Packers were awarded their first of three consecutive NFL titles with such Hall of Fame players as halfback Johnny McNally (also known as Johnny Blood), quarterback Arnie Herber, tackle Cal Hubbard, and guard Mike Michalske. But the club, which had survived financial troubles in 1922, nearly folded when a spectator won a five-thousand-dollar court verdict after falling out of the stands. Green Bay businessmen saved the franchise for end Don Hutson, who had been an All-America end at Alabama, to lead it to NFL championships in 1936, 1939, and 1944.

But by 1958 the Packers had dwindled into one of the NFL's worst teams. They were searching for a man to take command not only of the team but also of the organization.

At the time Lombardi was the New York Giants' offensive coach. In college he had been a guard at Fordham, one of the "Seven Blocks of Granite" built in 1937 by Frank Leahy, then an assistant coach there. The other linemen were Leo Paquin, Ed Franco, Nat Pierce, Alex Wojciechowicz (later a Hall of Fame center and linebacker for the Philadelphia Eagles), Al Barbartsky, and Johnny Druze.

Lombardi's coaching career began at St. Cecilia's High School in Englewood, New Jersey, where he won six state titles. He then joined Colonel Red Blaik's staff at Army before being hired by the Giants in 1954.

After five years as a Giant assistant under Jim Lee Howell, the then forty-five-year-old Lombardi enjoyed the challenge of trying to turn the Packers into a contender, if not preserving a franchise that might be moved to another city if the team did not succeed quickly. In his first game, the Packers upset the rival Bears, 9–6. When the season ended, the Packers had a respectable 7–5 record, the first time they had finished above .500 since 1947. Most of the players were holdovers from the previous season when the Packers had a 1–10–1 record, the worst in the NFL. The difference obviously was Lombardi's coaching.

"I demand a commitment to excellence and to victory," Lombardi once said, "and that is what life is all about."

Although his Packer players didn't always appreciate Lombardi's "commitment to excellence" during their punishing practice sessions, they cherished the victories that his repetition of practice plays created. To their coach, once a Latin teacher at St. Cecilia's, coaching was teaching. And in teaching, repetition is necessary until the students absorb the lesson. Lombardi applied that teaching philosophy to football.

"Do it again," he would say after a play in practice. "Do it again until we get it right."

Jim Taylor (31) gallops behind Jerry Kramer (64) and Fuzzy Thurston (63) following a play-action handoff from quarterback Bart Starr (15).

Of all the plays that the Packers did, again and again, the "sweep" was Lombardi's favorite. In the sweep the two guards, Jerry Kramer and Fuzzy Thurston, pulled out of the line and led the blocking around end for halfback Paul Hornung, who also was following another blocker, fullback Jim Taylor.

That sweep had been in coaches' playbooks for decades. But as the Packers rolled to one championship after another, it became known as the Green Bay Sweep, the trademark of Lombardi's teams.

Hornung, called "Golden Boy" because of his blond curly hair, had been the 1956 Heisman Trophy winner as a Notre Dame quarterback. With the Packers he started out as a quarterback.

But when Lombardi arrived in Green Bay, he switched Hornung to halfback and depended on Starr at quarterback.

Following the Packers' NFL championship in 1965, the NFL agreed to an eventual total merger with the American Football League. In the process, Super Bowl I was created—the first meeting of the NFL and AFL champions.

Paul Hornung dives across the goal line for another Packer touchdown.

The AFL had begun play as a rival league in 1960 in eight cities—New York, Boston, Buffalo, Dallas, Houston, Denver, Oakland, and Los Angeles—but within three years, two teams had been transplanted. The Chargers went from Los Angeles to San Diego; the Dallas Texans moved to Kansas City and were renamed the Chiefs. Then in 1966, the Miami Dolphins were organized; in 1968 the Cincinnati Bengals would be added. The AFL teams also were competing with the NFL teams for the best college talent.

As the salaries and bonuses soared higher and higher, club owners in both leagues agreed to merge the teams into one NFL, which would begin with the 1970 season. But in the few years before that, they would play the championship game and work together on a common draft of college players.

That first Super Bowl was played on January 15, 1967, as the finale of the 1966 season. As NFL champions again, the Packers opposed the Kansas City Chiefs, who had won the AFL title, at the Los Angeles Coliseum. In the days prior to that long-awaited confrontation, Lombardi was obviously much more tense than he had been for any other game as the Packers' coach.

"You're not only representing the Green Bay Packers," he told his players, "but the entire National Football League."

After struggling to a 14–10 lead at halftime, the Packers exploded for a 35–10 victory. Starr completed 16 of 23 passes for 260 yards. Max McGee, a long-time Packer wide receiver, came off the bench to replace Boyd Dowler, injured early in the game. McGee, who had caught only 3 passes all season, grabbed 7 for 138 yards and 2 touchdowns. Early in the second half, safety Willie Wood intercepted one of Len Dawson's passes to set up the Packer touchdown that broke the game open.

During the postgame interview Lombardi was asked to compare the Chiefs to other NFL teams.

"The Chiefs are a good team," he finally blurted, "but they don't compare with the top teams in the NFL. Dallas is a better team. Four or five NFL teams could have beaten the Chiefs . . ."

But later Lombardi was disturbed that he had been that blunt about the Chiefs in comparing them to NFL teams. "I wish I could get my words back," he said. "It was the wrong thing to say, the wrong thing. I came off as an ungracious winner."

The next year the Packers won Super Bowl II, 33–14, over the Oakland Raiders. It would be Lombardi's last game as their coach. Two weeks earlier the Packers had won what is now known as the National Football Conference title for the third consecutive year. In the final seconds of a game played in thirteen-degrees-below-zero weather at Lambeau Field in Green Bay, the Packers had edged the Cowboys, 21–17, in the final seconds when Starr barged into the end zone from the 1-yard line behind Jerry Kramer's block.

During the Packers' last time-out Lombardi had chosen to go for the touchdown and victory rather than try for a point-blank field goal that would have forced sudden-death overtime.

"If you can't run the ball in there in a moment of crisis like that," Lombardi said, "you don't deserve to win. These decisions don't come from the mind, they come from the gut."

His decision to leave the sideline and concentrate on his role as the Packers' general manager came from the gut, too. But shortly after the 1968 season ended, with the Packers having slipped under coach Phil Bengtson to a 6–7–1 record, Lombardi moved to Washington as the Redskins' part-owner, executive vice president, and coach.

Bart Starr (15) puts Packers in Super Bowl II behind guard Jerry
Kramer's block in the last seconds of NFL championship game.

"I miss the fire on Sunday," he explained.

By that Lombardi meant that he had missed the thrill of the game that a coach has. In his first season with the Redskins, he lifted them to a 7–5–2 record. But in the months that followed, he was stricken with cancer. Unable even to attend training camp, he died on September 3, 1970, shortly before the season was to open. But to the end he never changed.

"Once when I visited him, my hair had gotten pretty long," Hornung later recalled. "He called me near the bed and he said, 'Hey, get a haircut.' "

By then a shaggy-haired quarterback, Joe Namath of the New York Jets, had taken over the Super Bowl stage. The Jets, originally known as the Titans, were one of the AFL's charter franchises in 1960. But with an underfinanced owner, Harry Wismer, the Titans struggled. Before the 1963 season the club was purchased by a group headed by Sonny Werblin, a show business impressario. Werblin hired Weeb Ewbank as coach, the team's nickname was changed to the Jets, and they moved into the brand-new Shea Stadium in 1964. Then Werblin really created headlines.

Outbidding the St. Louis Cardinals of the NFL, the Jets signed Namath, who grew up in Beaver Falls, Pennsylvania, and had been a quarterback at Alabama, to a $427,000 contract. That was a dazzling amount of money at the time, especially for a rookie who needed a knee operation.

Not that Namath considered himself to be a risk. When he arrived in New York for the operation, he attended an informal get-together that Werblin had arranged with several New York sportswriters. Just stop by, Werblin told them, meet the $427,000

Joe Namath, the Jets' quarterback who established the AFL's credibility.

Joe Namath was called "an almost perfect passer" by Vince Lombardi.

quarterback, and maybe ask him a question. One sportswriter did.

"Joe," he said, "suppose you don't make it—what happens to the money?"

Namath stared at the sportswriter and replied firmly, "I'll make it."

Namath made it. In his third season, 1967, he was the first passer in pro football history to throw for more than 4,000 yards. To be exact, his total was 4,007 yards. At the time skeptics thought that Namath was merely a product of the AFL, that he really wasn't good enough to make it big in the NFL, but Vince Lombardi was not among the skeptics.

"Joe Namath," said Lombardi early in 1968, "is an almost perfect passer."

When the Jets qualified for Super Bowl III against the Baltimore Colts, skeptics still doubted Namath's skill. But he didn't doubt it. In the days before that game, he insisted that the upstart AFL had more good quarterbacks than the NFL establishment did.

"We've got better quarterbacks in our league," he said. "John Hadl [San Diego Chargers], Daryle Lamonica [Oakland Raiders], myself, and Bob Griese [Miami Dolphins]."

Namath also put down Earl Morrall, who had been the Colts' quarterback in the absence of the injured Johnny Unitas, thereby annoying Colts' coach Don Shula and his entire squad. On the Thursday night before Super Bowl III, while accepting a Miami Touchdown Club award as pro football's outstanding player that season, Namath made a short speech. In it he talked about the upcoming Super Bowl.

"We're going to win Sunday," he said, "I'll guarantee you."

In the game on Sunday, he made good his guarantee. The Jets won, 16–7, astonishing not only the Colts but also the entire NFL establishment.

"We showed a lot of people they were wrong," Namath said in the locker room. "Beautiful."

The next year the Kansas City Chiefs stunned the Minnesota Vikings, 23–7, in Super Bowl IV. Suddenly the AFL and the NFL were tied two apiece in the four Super Bowl games as they awaited the 1970 season. The twenty-six teams would then be realigned into two thirteen-team conferences, the NFC and the AFC, each with three divisions. The merger was complete. In the process Joe Namath had emerged as one of the most controversial players in football history, and Vince Lombardi had emerged as a legend.

MODERN TIMES

Bear Bryant and the Super Bowl

In the Alabama football office, Coach Paul (Bear) Bryant dialed the telephone number for Auburn University, the Crimson Tide's state rival. Bryant wanted to talk to the Auburn coach, but when the switchboard operator took the call, she glanced at her wristwatch. It was shortly after seven o'clock in the morning.

"I'm sorry," the operator said, "but there's nobody in the coach's office yet."

"What's the matter?" Bryant asked. "Don't your people take football seriously?"

Few people have taken football as seriously as Bear Bryant did. When he finally retired at age sixty-nine after his 'Bama team concluded its 1982 season by winning the Liberty Bowl game, he had more victories than any other coach in college football history—323 against only 85 losses and 17 ties. But on January 26, 1983, he died suddenly of a heart attack.

"Football is my life," the coach in the houndstooth hat often said. "If I retired, I'd be dead in a week."

As it turned out, he was dead in a month. But like Amos Alonzo Stagg, Pop Warner, Knute Rockne, George Halas, and Vince Lombardi, Bryant will be remembered as long as football is played, especially by his Alabama followers. The day he was buried, thousands lined the sixty miles of highway from Tuscaloosa, the site of a memorial service at a Methodist church near the Alabama campus, to a Birmingham cemetery. He was respected as a tough coach who transferred that toughness to his relatively small, fast players. When he was coaching at Kentucky, before moving on to Texas A & M and then to Alabama, one of his primary projects was harassing a big tackle, Bob Gain, to develop his potential. Gain eventually did just that with the Cleveland Browns, emerging as an All-Pro. While serving in the Army during the Korean conflict, Gain wrote Bryant a letter.

"I love you tonight," that letter said in part, "for what I used to hate you for."

College and high school graduates usually agree that their best teachers were the ones who worked them the hardest. And to Bryant a football coach was simply a "teacher, but he better be a leader, too." He'd better have some good players as well. Bryant had good players. He developed several outstanding NFL quarterbacks, notably Joe Namath, George Blanda, Ken Stabler, Vito (Babe) Parilli, and Richard Todd. He also coached Ray Perkins, a wide receiver who went on to coach the New York Giants before the Bear chose him as his successor at Alabama.

As the Bear, Bryant had one of America's most famous sports nicknames. He was a big man, at 6-4 and more than 200 pounds, but he earned his nickname for a dare, not for his size.

Growing up in Morro Bottom, Arkansas, one of eleven children in a poor farm family, he attended nearby Fordyce High School, where he played football. One day he walked into the town of Fordyce with his best friends, the Jordan twins. They were going

In his houndstooth hat, Paul Bryant was a Bear on the Alabama sidelines.

to the movies at what he called a "picture theater" when they noticed a poster. It offered a dollar for each minute anybody wrestled a real bear inside the theater, owned by a Mr. Smith.

"They egged me on," he later recalled, referring to the twins, "and Mr. Smith lined it up with the fellow who had the bear. Mr. Smith agreed to let me and my friends into the picture free."

Inside the theater he was relieved to see that the bear was somewhat scrawny. Although he wrestled it to the floor, the bear bit his ear. He later went to collect his money, but the man with the bear had skipped town.

"All I ever got out of it," Bryant often said, chuckling, "was a nickname."

But that nickname enhanced his reputation as a football player. In high school he was a tackle; at Alabama he played end. The other end was Don Hutson, who went on to make NFL history with the Packers as a pass receiver. Bear Bryant went on to coaching. His teams were awarded six national championships and played in twenty-six consecutive bowl games. He would view practice from a high tower where a metal chain was hooked across the entrance to the stairway.

"Whenever the chain hit the pipe," Ray Perkins recalled, "we knew he was on the way down to chew out somebody."

Every so often Bryant would be so displeased, he would tell a player to get dressed and go home and tell his mother and father exactly why he had been sent home.

"Coach Bryant," said Perkins, "was always aware of what he called mamas and papas. He always encouraged his players to write their mamas and papas at least once a week."

During the last years of Bear Bryant's career as a coach, another career was just starting, that of Herschel Walker, a University of Georgia running back. As a junior, Walker was voted the 1982 Heisman Trophy as the nation's outstanding college player. In three years he rushed for a total of 5,259 yards in 994 carries, a remarkable 5.3-yard average. He scored 52 touchdowns.

"Herschel is the greatest running back I've ever seen," said Fran Tarkenton, a former Georgia quarterback who set several NFL passing records with the Minnesota Vikings. "He's unbelievable."

"He's the greatest football player in America," said Johnny Majors, the University of Tennessee's head coach. "He's one of the few that God puts on this green earth every now and then."

But with another year of eligibility remaining, Walker chose to join the New Jersey Generals of the United States Football League, a new organization which began in 1983 with a spring schedule. Walker signed a reported $5 million contract, which put him and the USFL into headlines. It also reflected the popularity of the NFL, which signed television contracts in 1982 with the CBS, NBC, and ABC networks for a total of $2.1 billion.

For the second time in fewer than ten years, a new pro league hoped to challenge the NFL; the World Football League had tried in 1974 and failed. The USFL folded in 1986, but its birth had been inspired by the NFL's success, particularly by the growth of the Super Bowl game into one of America's biggest sports spectacles.

Prior to the 1985 season, thirteen of the last fourteen Super Bowl games were swept by five teams—the Pittsburgh Steelers with four championships; the Raiders of Oakland and Los Angeles with three; the Dallas Cowboys, the Miami Dolphins, and the San Francisco 49ers with two each.

During 1985, Herschel Walker joined Eric Dickerson and O.J. Simpson
as the only pro running backs to rush for more than 2,000 yards in a season.

The success of those five teams prompted a familiar question—are the players of today better than the players of the past? The usual answer is that today's players are bigger, stronger, and faster. Through the years the improvement in coaching techniques also has created a smarter player. But for all that, it is difficult to compare players or teams of different eras. Any player or any team can only truly be judged against its current competition and the standards of the time. But to be considered among the best of any era, a player or a team must perform at a winning level consistently over a period of time.

For those reasons the Steelers of the seventies, with their four Super Bowl championships in six years, deserve to be rated among the best teams in football history.

The success of the Steelers had begun with the toss of a coin. In the NFL draft of college players each year, the first choice goes to the team that had the worst record the previous season. According to most NFL scouts in 1970, the first choice was obvious. It would be Terry Bradshaw, a husky quarterback out of a small college, Louisiana Tech, who resembled a blond Li'l Abner, the comic book character. But during the 1969 season, both the Steelers and the Bears had the worst record: 1 victory, 13 defeats. To determine the first choice in the draft, Commissioner Pete Rozelle tossed a coin.

The Steelers won the toss.

As a rookie Bradshaw struggled, as did the Steelers, a team that had struggled throughout its history. Of all the NFL owners, Art Rooney of the Steelers was perhaps the most beloved—also the most beleaguered. After the 1968 season he had known it was time to change coaches again. He had hired Chuck Noll, once a guard for Paul Brown in Cleveland, at the time an assistant coach under Don Shula with the Colts.

In their first season under Noll, the Steelers had that 1–13 record. But in retrospect it enabled the Steelers to obtain the passer who would turn their franchise around.

By the 1972 season Bradshaw had not yet completely established himself as the Steeler quarterback, but he was on his way. He also was joined by Franco Harris, a rookie fullback from Penn State who would gallop through opposing defensive units for more than a decade. Harris's most memorable moment occurred as a rookie after he, Bradshaw, and defensive tackle Mean Joe Greene had helped put the Steelers in the NFL playoffs for the first time in their history.

In the opening playoff game against the Oakland Raiders at Three Rivers Stadium, the Steelers were losing, 7–6, with only twenty seconds remaining. On fourth down at their own 40-yard line, Bradshaw threw a desperation pass toward halfback John (Frenchy) Fuqua, who went up for the ball with Jack Tatum, a Raider safety. The ball rebounded to Harris, who caught it at his shoe tops and ran untouched into the end zone. Touchdown, and the Steelers won, 13–7.

At the time the NFL rule was that a pass could not ricochet from one offensive player to another offensive player. But the officials ruled that the ball had rebounded off Tatum, not Fuqua.

Harris's catch was dubbed the "immaculate reception." It put the Steelers into the AFC championship game, which they lost to the Miami Dolphins. But two seasons later, on January 12, 1975, the Steelers won their first NFL title for Art Rooney, conquering the Minnesota Vikings, 16–6, in Super Bowl IX. They repeated

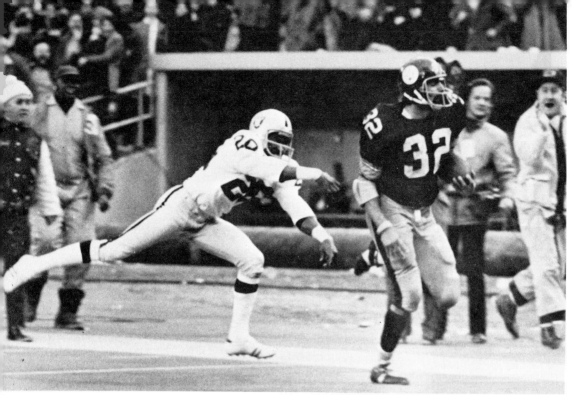

Franco Harris scoring after his "immaculate reception."

the next year, 21–17, over the Dallas Cowboys as wide receiver
Lynn Swann made several acrobatic catches, including one for a
64-yard touchdown.

Bradshaw, Harris, Swann, and their Steel Curtain defense also
won Super Bowl XIII, 35–31, over the Cowboys and Super Bowl
XIV, 31–19, over the Los Angeles Rams.

The Cowboys also won the Super Bowl twice, prompting the
franchise to call itself "America's team," a phrase disputed by
several NFL rivals. For all the debate, the Cowboys indeed were a
popular team with a popular quarterback. Roger Staubach had
joined the Cowboys after four years in the Navy, some of it in
Vietnam as a supply officer. As a junior at the Naval Academy, he
had won the Heisman Trophy in 1963. Eight seasons later he led
the Cowboys to a 24–3 victory over the Dolphins in Super Bowl

VI, completing 12 of 19 passes for 119 yards and 2 touchdowns. The next day he was awarded the keys to a new car by *Sport* magazine as the game's most valuable player. In his acceptance speech he displayed his sense of humor as well as his spiritual outlook.

"I enjoy my Christian ideals," he said. "I believe there's something greater than what we're here for."

Asked if there were zone defenses "up there," he laughed and replied, "From what I understand, every pass is a touchdown up there." Reminded that if you were a defensive back, every pass wouldn't be a touchdown, he smiled.

Roger Staubach of the Cowboys dodging away from a Redskin pursuer.

"Up there," he said, "they don't have any defensive backs."

Six years later, in Super Bowl XII after the 1977 season, Staubach guided the Cowboys to a 27–10 triumph over the Denver Broncos. Ironically the Broncos' quarterback, Craig Morton, had been Staubach's predecessor before Coach Tom Landry decided to go with the former naval officer with the quick arm, the quick feet, and the quick brain. As the Cowboys' coach since the team began operating in the 1960 season, Landry occasionally had been hounded by having to choose between two capable quarterbacks—Don Meredith and Morton in the late sixties, Morton and Staubach in the early seventies, Danny White and Gary Hogeboom in 1984.

On the sideline in his snap-brim hat, Landry projected a sense of calm leadership that reflected his complete absorption in the game until his unceremonious dismissal early in 1989.

"Leadership," he once said, "is a matter of having people look at you and gain confidence, seeing how you react. If you're in control, they're in control. It's not that I'm unemotional or computerized. But as a coach I seldom see a play as others do. If it's a pass play, I'm trying to read the opposing team's pass defense. I usually don't even see the ball in the air. If it's a running play, I'm looking at the point of attack where the key block is. I have to know whether a play broke down because of our blocking or because the other team changed its defense. If you were to see me as a cheerleader, that would mean I was only watching instead of thinking."

His players treated Landry with fond respect, knowing that a mistake would provoke the coach's famous stare, whether in practice or a game.

Tom Landry's leader-
ship philosophy:
"Having people look
at you and gain
confidence."

"One time I messed up an assignment," safety Cliff Harris
once confessed. "I could feel his eyes on me like a ray gun from
fifty yards away."

Of all the Cowboy running backs, Tony Dorsett developed into
the most dependable as well as the most gifted. But as a rookie
who had won the Heisman Trophy at Pitt, he did not open the
1977 season as a starter. Realizing that Dorsett was annoyed,
Landry called him aside and explained that a Cowboy rookie had
to know the team's complex offensive system completely before
being trusted as a starter, especially as a pass receiver.

Tony Dorsett of the Cowboys was a Heisman Trophy winner at Pitt.

"I realize that, coach," Dorsett said, "but I can catch 'em on Sunday."

"First," the coach said softly, "you've got to catch 'em in practice."

Landry did what no other coach has done—win the Super Bowl six years apart with two virtually different teams. Other coaches whose teams won the Super Bowl more than once have done it mostly with the same players. But the distinction of winning the Super Bowl to complete a perfect season is held by only one coach. Under the firm gaze of Don Shula, the Miami Dolphins swept through the 1972 season with a 17–0 record, finishing with a 14–7 victory over the Washington Redskins in Super Bowl VII. The next year the Dolphins repeated in Super Bowl VIII, 24–7, over the Vikings.

In assessing the best NFL coaches of the modern era, John Madden, himself the coach of the Super Bowl XI champion Oakland Raiders and later a television analyst, chose Shula as the best.

"Shula has won with different teams in different cities," Madden said. "He won in Baltimore with Johnny Unitas at quarterback, and he won there with Earl Morrall at quarterback when Unitas was hurt. Then he took over a team in Miami that had Larry Csonka and Bob Griese and he won the Super Bowl twice. Then he developed a completely different team in 1982 that lost, 27–17, to the Washington Redskins in Super Bowl XVII with David Woodley at quarterback. Then he inserted Dan Marino at quarterback the next year."

Csonka, the Nagurski-like fullback of the Dolphins' two Super Bowl champions, remembered Shula's arrival at Miami in 1970 when a labor dispute delayed the opening of the NFL training camps.

"When we finally got to camp," Csonka said, "Shula told us, 'We've got to make up for lost time. We're going to have four workouts a day.' We had two in the morning at eight and eleven, another in the afternoon at two, another at seven at night until the sun went down. Sometimes we even kept practicing in the dark until he was happy. No other team in pro football ever had four workouts a day before or since."

In one of those workouts, Csonka was lined up as a dummy blocker for Griese in a passing drill.

Suddenly the big fullback heard Shula shouting at him from forty yards away. "Csonka," the coach was yelling, "what are you doing?"

At first Csonka had no idea why the coach was shouting at him. But in another moment he knew.

"You lined up a step too wide," Shula yelled. "If a linebacker had been coming, you'd have been too far out to block him."

Thinking back to that moment, Csonka once said, "Right then I knew I'd better concentrate every second." That's the type of concentration Shula demanded, the type that produced that perfect season. In addition to Csonka and Griese, the 1972 Dolphin team alternated Jim Kiick and Eugene (Mercury) Morris at halfback, had Paul Warfield at wide receiver, and had what was nicknamed its "No Name" defensive unit, even though it had two All-Pro performers: middle linebacker Nick Buoniconti and safety Dick Anderson. But even when the unbeaten Dolphins were preparing for the Super Bowl game, Shula didn't let them lose their concentration.

"All those games we've won," he told his players, "they won't mean anything if we lose this game."

The Dolphins won and were champions again the next year. Don Shula had established himself as one of the NFL's best coaches. But another coach, O. A. (Bum) Phillips, then with the Houston Oilers, put Shula's skill in its proper perspective.

Don Shula coached the 1972 Dolphins to a perfect 17–0 record.

"Shula can take his'n and beat your'n," Phillips said in his Texas twang, "or he can take your'n and beat his'n."

During a ten-season span from 1971 through 1980 in which four teams swept all the Super Bowl games, the Oakland Raiders were the only one to win with two different coaches: John Madden and Tom Flores. Madden's team routed the Minnesota Vikings, 32–14, in Super Bowl XI as quarterback Ken Stabler guided an offense that rolled up 429 yards, including 137 rushing yards by halfback Clarence Davis. Four years later, Flores's team stunned the Philadelphia Eagles, 27–10, as quarterback Jim Plunkett, discarded by the San Francisco 49ers after having been traded by the New England Patriots, threw 3 touchdown passes. He completed 13 of 21 passes for 261 yards.

Flores's team was the first to win the Super Bowl after having qualified for the NFL playoffs as a wild-card team, meaning one of the two second-place teams in each conference that qualify to compete in the playoffs.

But the Raiders' success always focused on Al Davis, their managing general partner. When he was hired as coach in 1963, the Raiders had been one of the AFL's worst teams. He quickly turned the Raiders into a winner. Named the AFL commissioner in 1966, he helped force the merger with the NFL, then returned to Oakland as the team's part-owner. He provided the team with a motto, "Pride and Poise," and a slogan, "The Dynamic Organization." In recent years, with the Raiders' move to Los Angeles, he added another slogan, "Commitment to Excellence."

"I always wanted to build the finest organization in sports," Davis has said. "And someday, in some way, I would be in control. I'd have the greatest players, the greatest coaches. We'd play the greatest games. And someone would say, 'That's the best organization in sports.' I wanted it to be the ultimate."

After the Raiders moved to Los Angeles, they also won Super Bowl XVIII, 38–9, over the Washington Redskins, who had defeated the Dolphins, 37–17, the year before. This time halfback Marcus Allen was the Raiders' star, rushing for 191 yards, including a startling 74-yard touchdown run that began to the left before he cut back up the middle. By then the Raiders were considered to be NFL rebels for having moved the franchise from Oakland to Los Angeles without the approval of the other NFL clubowners. When the NFL objected, Davis went to court. After a long trial, a federal jury granted him the right to move without NFL approval. In their silver-and-black uniforms, the Raiders had the look of the bad guys in old movie Westerns. But to their followers they were the good guys who had won three Super Bowl games in a span of eight seasons.

The 49ers soon emerged as a four-time Super Bowl champion while their quarterback, Joe Montana, was chosen as the game's most valuable player a record three times.

Three years after defeating the Cincinnati Bengals, 26–21, at the Pontiac (Michigan) Silverdome, the 49ers dominated the Dolphins, 38–16, in Super Bowl XIX at Palo Alto, California, only a few miles from their training base. Over the next three seasons the Chicago Bears and the New York Giants each would earn Super Bowl rings for the first time and the Redskins for the second time. But then Montana guided the 49ers to two more titles. His 10-yard touchdown pass to John Taylor in the waning seconds at Joe Robbie Stadium in Miami created a 20–16 comeback victory over the Bengals in Super Bowl XXIII, and his five touchdown passes riddled the Denver Broncos, 55–10.

With his success and flair for the dramatic, Montana was touted as arguably the best quarterback in history, while the 49er coach in three of those triumphs, Bill Walsh, earned his niche among the best coaches.

The slim, silver-haired Walsh was known as a sculptor of quarterbacks. In a decade as an assistant coach with the Bengals and Chargers, he developed Ken Anderson and Dan Fouts; in his two

Joe Montana was the "perfect quarterback" for Bill Walsh's 49er offense.

years as head coach at Stanford University, he polished both Guy Benjamin and Steve Dils into the nation's leading college passer; when he took command of the 49ers in 1978, his offense enabled Steve DeBerg to complete 347 passes, then a NFL record. Halfway through the 1980 seasons Walsh decided that Montana was his new quarterback.

"Joe is the quarterback of the future," Walsh said the next year. "He's got a fine arm and he's got the quickness of feet that Joe Namath had."

Montana fulfilled Walsh's prophecy. Prior to the 1991 season, he had developed into the leading passer in NFL history, according to the NFL's complex statistical ratings. But just as he was credited by Walsh for having the intelligence and the athletic ability that has enabled him to accomplish what he has, the former Notre Dame quarterback credited the 49er coach with having brought out the best in him.

"If something goes wrong," Montana once said, "the coach tells me right there on the sideline what I should've done. I don't always agree, but when I see the films, I realize he was right. He's always right."

The best coaches usually are. After Walsh left the 49ers for the television booth, one of his assistants, George Seifert, took over as head coach and charted the record 55–10 rout of the Broncos for the 49ers' fourth Super Bowl ring. But just when the 49ers were dreaming of a third consecutive title, the Giants stunned them, 15–13, in the National Conference championship game on Matt Bahr's 42-yard field goal as time expired. The Giants prevailed, 20–19, in Super Bowl XXV when a 47-yard field-goal attempt by Scott Norwood of the Buffalo Bills drifted wide as time expired.

With two Super Bowl rings in five seasons, Bill Parcells was considered the best coach in the long history of that flagship franchise before he suddenly resigned in 1991. But his legacy lingers.

"Give 'em a good design," Parcells liked to say, meaning the game plan, "and get 'em to play hard."

It sounds simple, but that philosophy also has been true of Bill Walsh and Don Shula, just as it was true of Amos Alonzo Stagg and Knute Rockne so many years ago. As football approaches the twenty-first century, it indeed has changed from 1869, when Rutgers and Princeton played that first game. But in the sense that the best coaches are still assembling the best teams, football has hardly changed at all.

PART TWO

In nine seasons, Jim Brown rushed an average of 104 yards per game.

RUNNING

"Eight Yards Might Not Seem Like Much"

To understand what it's like to be a running back, listen to Larry Csonka, who has explained it as well as anyone ever has.

"To gain eight yards might not seem like much," he once said, "until you put eleven defensive players in those eight yards."

Big Zonk, as he was known, was the 240-pound fullback on the 1972 Miami Dolphins who won Super Bowl VII to complete a perfect 17–0 record. But at any level of football competition, eight yards on a running play represents a substantial gain. For all the emphasis today on passing, running (or rushing, as the statisticians prefer to describe it) is considered by many coaches to be even more important to a team's offense.

In order for a passing attack to succeed, a team usually must "establish," as coaches like to say, its running game. Without an effective running game, it's easier for an opposing team to gear its defense to stop the pass.

Even though Walter Payton has surpassed Jim Brown's career total of 12,312 rushing yards in NFL regular-season competition, the onetime Cleveland Browns' fullback remains the standard by whom all ball carriers are measured. Although Brown stopped playing in 1965 after only nine seasons so he could pursue a career as a motion picture actor, he still holds three of the most significant NFL records—126 touchdowns, a 5.22-yard average per rush, and a 104.3-yard average per game. Most running backs never have a 100-yard game, but Jim Brown *averaged* more than 100 yards per game throughout his career. He also *averaged* more than 5 yards per carry.

With a 6-2, 228-pound physique that tapered to a 32-inch waist, Brown blended power and speed as no other running back ever has. When a yard or two was needed for a first down, he would blast through the middle of the line. If he suddenly had some room beyond the line of scrimmage, he would take off for a long gain, often outrunning some defensive backs. From the time he joined the Browns out of Syracuse University in 1957, he was the backbone of the Browns' offense for nine seasons—so much so that the Cleveland coach, Paul Brown, occasionally was criticized for using him too much.

"But when you have a big gun," the coach said, "you shoot it."

Despite his heavy-duty role, Jim Brown never missed a game because of injury. If anything he seemed to inflict more punishment on tacklers than he received.

"All you can do," Sam Huff, the Giants' middle linebacker, once said, "is grab him, hold on, and wait for help."

That same feeling has been shared by tacklers trying to stop Walter Payton, the Chicago Bears' running back. Entering the 1985 season, Payton had rushed for a record total of 13,309 yards, a tribute not only to his development of his gifts as a runner but also to his dedication to conditioning his body. In the off-season, he works out as much as six or seven hours a day to keep himself strong, especially his legs.

"When I don't work out, I get bored, restless, and lazy," he has said. "I lose my edge, and that's one thing I can't afford to lose."

Payton's continual workouts have hardened his 5-11, 202-pound physique into what appears to be a statue of what the perfectly proportioned athlete should look like. Fred O'Connor, a Bears' assistant coach, once described Payton's physique.

"God must've taken a chisel," O'Connor said, "and decided, 'I'm going to make a halfback.' "

During his career at Jackson (Mississippi) State, a predominantly black school, Payton scored 464 points, a college record. In addition to his 65 touchdowns, he kicked 5 field goals and 59 extra points. He rushed for 3,563 yards, caught 27 passes for another 474 yards, completed 14 of 19 passes for 4 touchdowns, averaged 43 yards on kickoff returns, and punted for a 39-yard average. For all that, he received little national publicity, and as a senior finished a distant twelfth in the Heisman Trophy voting. But the NFL scouts knew all about him. He was signed by the Bears and began playing for them in the 1975 season.

"When I came into the NFL, on a scale of one to ten, I was only a five," Payton said during the 1981 season. "Now, maybe because of experience and all that, maybe I've become an eight."

Payton was underestimating himself. Like most running backs, he knows he can't do much without good blocking. But once sprung beyond the line of scrimmage, he has the speed and the strength to dazzle defensive backs. In a tough 10–7 victory over the Vikings in 1977, he piled up 275 yards for an NFL single-game record.

"They opened the holes," Payton said of his blockers after that game, "and I just ran."

Walter Payton of the Bears broke Jim Brown's career rushing record.

In a sense that's true. The best running backs operate mostly on instinct. In taking a handoff or a pitchout from the quarterback, a running back peers out from under his helmet to see if his blockers are creating a hole in the line for him according to the design of the play—the point of attack, as coaches call it. If that hole is there, he will run through it, then look to see where the linebackers and the defensive backs are. By now the running back is no longer thinking. Instead he is reacting to what's in front of him—darting one way, dodging another.

"You don't have time to think things out when you're running, you just do it," Franco Harris has said. "If you stop to think, it's usually too late to do anything."

Harris rushed for 12,120 regular-season yards. But counting postseason competition, the fullback on the Steelers' four Super Bowl championship teams had 13,676 yards. In his nineteen playoff, championship, and Super Bowl games, he rushed for a total of 1,556 yards. If a yard is a yard is a yard, in the postseason as well as the regular season, Harris is the NFL's all-time leader: counting the postseason, he was responsible for 16,700 yards in what is known as all-purpose yardage, including 2,791 as a pass receiver and 233 early in his career on kickoff returns.

Harris grew up in Mount Holly, New Jersey, not far from Fort Dix, where his father was stationed as an Army sergeant. His father had met his mother during World War II in Italy, where she then lived. Because of his mother's Italian ancestry, Harris inspired Pittsburgh fans to organize "Franco's Italian Army" during his rookie season in 1972. He endured as one of the Steelers' most popular players for more than a decade.

As a runner, Harris, a first-round draft choice out of Penn

State, had a tiptoe style, unusual for a fullback. Instead of slamming at the line, as most fullbacks do, the 6-2, 225-pound Harris often changed direction. Sometimes he seemed to run sideways until he found room to run. That style helped him score 100 regular-season touchdowns, fifth among NFL players behind Jim Brown, Lenny Moore, John Riggins, and Don Hutson.

Harris's style is added proof that the best running backs are born, not made.

"With a runner," says John Robinson, the Rams' coach, "you can really hurt him when you begin to coach him where to run the football. To be a good runner, he's got to be able to do things you can't coach. That's why a good running back can play well as a rookie in the NFL right away; he doesn't have to learn that much like a quarterback does. With a good running back, all he really has to do is carry the ball. His instincts do the rest."

Of the young running backs, Eric Dickerson of the Rams is among the best. As a rookie in 1983, he rushed for 1,808 yards, lifting the Rams into the playoffs. Tall, fast, and strong at 6-3 and 220, he carried the ball 393 times that year, an NFL record. In 1984, he rushed for 2,105 yards, breaking the record of 2,003 set by O.J. Simpson.

"Dickerson is the best I've ever seen, and I mean *ever,*" Simpson, himself considered one of the best running backs ever, has said. "He has the speed, he has the size, and he has the moves. He also has the coach. John Robinson knows how to use a running back. When he [Robinson] was at Southern Cal, he had an offense that enabled Marcus Allen to get 2,342 yards his senior year—that's unbelievable. Dickerson is in the right environment and in the right system with the Rams."

Simpson, of course, was arguably one of the most spectacular running backs himself. After winning the Heisman Trophy in 1968 at Southern Cal, he joined the Buffalo Bills as the first choice in the NFL draft.

During the 1973 season Simpson broke loose for his 2,003 yards, then the regular-season NFL record. Before his final game that year, against the Jets at Shea Stadium in New York, he needed 61 yards to break Jim Brown's record of 1,863 yards, set in 1963. Despite a snowstorm, Simpson galloped for 200 yards. At the news conference later, he arrived with the other ten members of the Bills' offensive unit.

"These are the cats who did the job all year," he said of his teammates. "It's their record as much as mine."

Simpson grew up in the Potrero Hill section of San Francisco, where he occasionally went to see the 49ers, the team with which he would end his NFL career. As a teenager in 1962 he watched Jim Brown rush for 135 yards and score two touchdowns against the 49ers in the Browns' 13–10 victory. After the game, Orenthal James Simpson collected discarded seat cushions, returning them to the concessionaire for five cents apiece. With fresh pocket money, he stopped at a nearby ice-cream store when Jim Brown walked in.

"You just wait till I get up there," Simpson said. "I'll break all your records."

Jim Brown laughed. So did O.J., who was playfully teasing Brown more than boasting of his own undeveloped skill. As it turned out, O.J. did break Brown's record for rushing yardage in one season. For his career Simpson accumulated 11,236 yards.

"O.J.," said Don Shula, the Dolphins' coach, "was the best pure runner of all time."

Simpson had a hesitant style. As he approached the line of

O.J. Simpson is "looking to see which way the linebacker is being blocked."

scrimmage, he seemed to be moving in slow motion, waiting to pick his hole. But as soon as he saw it, he was through it in a flash, often on his way to a long gain. Like most teams, the Bills usually ran to their right, meaning behind the right side of the offensive line—the right guard, the right tackle, and the tight end (who usually lines up "tight" next to the right tackle).

"Going to the right," Simpson once explained, "I'm generally looking to see which way the linebacker on that side is being blocked. If he's being blocked inside, I'll go outside; if he's being blocked outside, I'll go inside. Once through the hole, I usually know where the strong safety is coming from, even if I can't see him. I just know where he *should* be. That's why I play better against good teams. They're more consistent on defense. They're easier to clock."

In recent years, several other running backs have put together Hall of Fame yardage—John Riggins, Tony Dorsett, Earl Campbell, to name three of Walter Payton's contemporaries.

At his best, Larry Csonka was a battering-ram fullback who enjoyed crashing into linemen and linebackers. He accumulated 8,081 yards, mostly with the Dolphins; his yardage with the Memphis Southmen of the World Football League is not counted by NFL statisticians. But just as Big Zonk defined running with his theory that "eight yards might not seem like much until you put eleven defensive players in those eight yards," he also defined what it takes for someone to be a running back at heart, to have the makings of a running back.

"Running backs have to be big and strong," he once said, "but they also have to enjoy the chase, like kids do. If you were a kid who loved to have people chase you, you've got the beginnings of

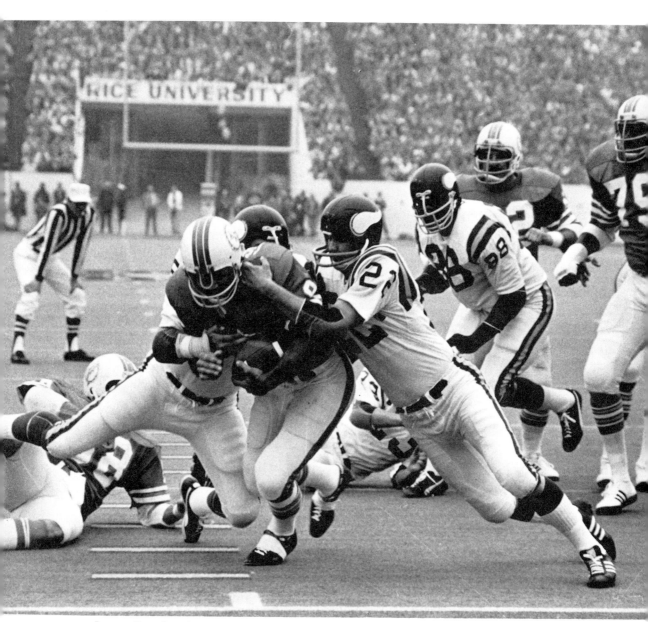

Larry Csonka slamming through Viking tacklers in Super Bowl VIII.

a running back. If you were scared of being chased, there's no way you could become one. It's an inner something that can't be changed. Show me a kid who's ten years old, and I'll tell you right away if he can be a running back. That doesn't mean he will be one, but I'll know if he's got the soul of a running back."

For a running back, whether he is in the NFL or is a youngster, the threat of a knee injury always lurks on the next play.

"Every running back," Csonka said, "is aware that he's running on ice. He never knows where the thin ice is, where the big injury is waiting for him. But inside himself a running back really believes that he can't be injured. He knows that he's going to have injuries, but never one that will really cripple him, never one that will finish him.

"As a kid I never thought about getting hurt. I ran through herds of cows. I ran through creeks. And if I fell down, I came up running. I never laid there moaning that I was hurt. When the other kids wouldn't run into the briar patch because they didn't want to get all scratched up, I never thought of being scratched up as being hurt."

Being hurt, according to Larry Csonka's philosophy, is the knee injury that shortened the career of halfback Gale Sayers.

As a Bears' rookie out of the University of Kansas in 1965, the 6-0, 200-pound Sayers was an instant All-Pro selection. During a 61–20 triumph over the 49ers that year, he scored 6 touchdowns for the Bears, tying the NFL record set by Ernie Nevers of the Chicago Cardinals in 1929 and equaled by Dub Jones of the Browns in 1951. Among his touchdowns that day, one was a 50-yard run from scrimmage, another was an 80-yard pass play, and a third was an 85-yard punt return.

During a 1968 game Sayers was tackled by Kermit Alexander, a 49er cornerback. His knee, which required surgery, was never the same after that. Although he would be named All-Pro in each of his first five seasons, the 1971 season was his last.

At his best Sayers was among football's most instinctive running backs. Avoiding tacklers, he seemed to slide sideways, then burst ahead at full speed. Watching films of his runs, teammates and opponents shook their head in disbelief at the running back that George Halas called "the best he had ever seen." And as the Papa Bear, one of the NFL's founders, Halas had seen them all, from Jim Thorpe and Red Grange to Jim Brown and Walter Payton.

Other old-timers insist that Hugh McElhenny, somewhat forgotten in recent years, was the best, especially during his peak seasons with the 49ers, beginning in 1952.

Out of the University of Washington, this 6-1, 198-pound halfback was virtually a tightrope walker with a football. His balance was remarkable as he weaved his way through tacklers, so many of whom he left grasping air instead of him. As a rookie, he averaged 7 yards a carry while rushing for 684 yards. After one of McElhenny's long runs, the 49er quarterback, Frankie Albert, shook his head.

"He's the king," Albert said, "the king of the runners."

From then on, the King was McElhenny's nickname. He accumulated 11,375 all-purpose yards as a runner, receiver, punt returner, and kickoff returner, including 5,281 rushing yards. Another teammate, quarterback Y.A. Tittle, labeled him "The finest running back I ever saw, there never was an open-field runner like him." Quite a career for someone who as a youngster had been confined to bed for five months and on crutches for an-

Hugh McElhenny, the 49er halfback who was "the King" of the runners.

other seven months due to an accident in which he had severed tendons of one foot on a broken milk bottle. In reflecting on his ability, he once described what it was like for him to be a running back.

"It's like walking down a dark alley," McElhenny said. "And then you see at the end of the alley a glimpse of light from the cross street—that's the goal line. You're desperately trying to get to the cross street, but on the way, even though the alley is so dark you can't see a thing, you sense a telegraph pole to your right, and you shy away from it. A few steps farther, you know there's a doorway with a man in it, even though you can't see him. You just feel it, so you turn away from that, too. Haven't you had that experience? I have. And then you're glad to reach that cross street with the bright lights—the goal line.''

McElhenny teamed in the 49er backfield with Joe Perry, a fullback who blasted for 9,723 yards. Teams seldom have two running backs of that quality. But the Packers of the Vince Lombardi era did—Jim Taylor at fullback and Paul Hornung at halfback.

Taylor, at 6-0 and 215 pounds, was a terror who enjoyed crashing into tacklers rather than avoiding them. One day when Lombardi asked why he didn't try to sidestep a tackler, Taylor replied, ''You've got to sting 'em, coach. If you give a guy a little blast, maybe next time he won't be so eager. You've got to make 'em respect you. You've got to punish them before they punish you. You've got to give more than you take.'' Taylor did, accumulating 8,597 career yards. Hornung, 6-3 and 210, a Heisman Trophy winner at Notre Dame, had only 3,711 rushing yards for the Packers, but he scored 62 touchdowns.

''Inside the 20-yard line, Hornung is one of the greatest I have ever seen,'' Lombardi once said. ''He smells the goal line.''

For a running back there is no higher compliment. For a running back the goal line is why he's out there carrying the ball.

PASSING

Three Seconds to Throw

Three seconds. Say them slowly. One . . . two . . . three. That's the amount of time that a passer usually has from the moment he takes the snap from the center, hurries back a few yards, searches for a receiver, and throws the football. Occasionally he might have a second or two more. Sometimes he might have even less than three seconds. But in timing a pass play, most coaches believe that a quarterback has no more than three seconds to throw the ball.

Any longer than that, a passer usually has been either tackled or forced to scramble, which means eluding tacklers while hoping to find an open receiver.

Three seconds. That's all. In a game passing is not like playing catch in the backyard. In a game passing is not only throwing the football to a receiver in less than three seconds but completing it for a gain. To do that on the NFL level, a quarterback must have several talents—a strong and accurate arm, quick footwork, intelligence in reading a defense, good vision in finding an open receiver, toughness in standing in there against the pass rush, and leadership in the clutch of a close game.

Of all those talents, however, the most important is a strong, accurate arm. Without it a player can't be a passer. That doesn't mean he can't be a good football player at another position. But if he is going to be a passer, he must have a strong, accurate arm.

Even in the NFL some passers have stronger arms than others. Terry Bradshaw, who led the Pittsburgh Steelers to four Super Bowl championships, had one of the NFL's strongest arms, if not the strongest. Husky at 6-3 and 210 pounds, he could throw a hard pass even with tacklers hanging on him. In assessing Bradshaw at the end of the Steeler quarterback's career, Al Davis, the overseer of the Los Angeles Raiders, called him "the most productive quarterback" in recent NFL history.

Not even Bradshaw, however, was an instantly productive quarterback. As a rookie he threw his short passes too hard. He had to learn how to throw a pass with what coaches call "touch," meaning lofting the ball just beyond the reach of a linebacker or floating it out to a running back on a screen play.

Bradshaw also had to learn how to read defenses, especially the zone defenses that are designed to confuse a quarterback. In a man-to-man defense, for example, a cornerback is assigned to cover a wide receiver anywhere in the field. But in a zone defense, a cornerback may cover a wide receiver for only a few strides; once the wide receiver leaves the cornerback's zone and enters another zone, another defensive back will cover him. In trying to look for a receiver in the mass of players between them, a quarterback also has to realize what type of zone defense the opposing team is using.

For a quarterback to do that quickly, almost instinctively, he needs experience. Bradshaw wasn't completely comfortable in reading defenses until 1974, the year the Steelers went on to win their first Super Bowl title.

Terry Bradshaw was the quarterback on four Super Bowl champions.

"In a game against the New England Patriots late that season," center Ray Mansfield once said, "Terry suddenly was in complete charge. He knew it and we knew it. That was the game when Terry really came of age, and so did our entire team."

Without a productive quarterback a team might win a few games. But it will never win a divisional championship, much less a Super Bowl game. One of the NFL's most productive quarterbacks was Otto Graham, who led the Cleveland Browns to three NFL titles and four All-America Football Conference championships as well as ten consecutive divisional titles from 1946 through 1955.

"For me, the key to reading defenses was reading the linebackers," Graham always said. "The linebackers are going to blitz or they're not."

Graham didn't have as strong an arm as some passers, but his arm was strong enough. And he was an exceptional athlete. While at Northwestern University he was chosen as an All-American in basketball as well as football. He later played pro basketball briefly.

"What helped me more than anything else in adjusting to the T-formation was the fact that I was a good basketball player," he said. "The mechanics of quarterbacking are the same as in basketball. The footwork and the pivoting are identical."

As a quarterback, Graham mastered the art of the pass to a wide receiver near the sideline.

"The secret is to have the receiver come back," he said. "You tell a guy to make a ninety-degree cut toward the sideline, but with his momentum he's actually still going downfield. By making the receiver cut back, he has the defender beaten by two steps. The defender is also blocked off by the receiver's body. I threw the ball in relation to where the defensive back was, not where the receiver was."

Thirty years after Graham stopped playing, he still held the NFL career record for the highest average gain as a passer, 8.63 yards. In his ten seasons with the Browns, he threw for 23,584 yards and 174 touchdowns. He also endeared himself to Coach Paul Brown because he seldom threw costly interceptions.

All coaches dislike having their passer intercepted because it turns over the ball to the opposing team. Occasionally an interception is run back for a touchdown. In his heyday as a coach, Brown complained about interceptions more than most coaches. If a passer repeatedly was intercepted, Brown didn't keep him long. Once, after trading a new quarterback, Brown had a simple explanation.

"That young man," he said, "did not understand how I feel about interceptions."

Brown apparently passed on his philosophy to Weeb Ewbank, once his offensive line coach with the Browns and later the head coach of the Baltimore Colts and the New York Jets. During Joe Namath's early years with the Jets, he had games where he was intercepted much too often, at least in Ewbank's judgment.

"Suppose," the coach was asked, "Namath keeps throwing all these interceptions?"

"In that case," Ewbank said quickly, "we'll just have to get rid of him."

The Jets didn't get rid of Namath, of course. He learned to throw fewer interceptions. When the Jets won Super Bowl III in a 16–7 upset of the Baltimore Colts, he completed 17 of 28 passes

Dolphin safety Jake Scott leaps for what a passer fears—an interception.

for 206 yards with no interceptions. But even the best passers have days when interceptions occur. In a 1970 game against the Chicago Bears, the Colts won, 21–20, even though Johnny Unitas threw five interceptions. When asked about the interceptions after that game, Unitas shrugged.

"They happen," he said.

Interceptions sometimes happen by accident—when a pass bounces off a receiver or a defensive player downfield, or when a pass is batted into the air by a defensive player even before it crosses the line of scrimmage. In fairness, an interception of that type is usually not the passer's fault. But in the statistics it is charged as an interception. To be a good passer, however, a quarterback should not be overly concerned with throwing interceptions. If he worries too much about being intercepted, he will not take the chances that a good passer should take. Ideally he should be careful in throwing a pass but not too careful; he must take a risk occasionally but not often.

Interceptions happen more often to passers who prefer to throw the ball far downfield, as Namath and Unitas did, rather than tossing short, safer passes.

In a 1972 game between the Jets and the Colts, Namath and Unitas accumulated 822 yards. While throwing for 6 touchdowns in a 44–34 victory, Namath produced 496 yards with only 15 completions in 28 attempts. In the final quarter he collaborated with wide receiver Rich Caster for a 79-yard touchdown. But Unitas' second touchdown pass narrowed the Jets' lead to 37–34 and inspired Namath.

"Waiting for the kickoff," Namath later explained, "I was thinking about another long pass to Caster on the first play, but I

Where's his receiver? Joe Namath throws against some huge pass rushers.

wasn't sure if I should risk it, only three points ahead. But then I said to myself, 'If you ain't confident, you don't belong here,' so I decided to score again quick."

On first down Namath threw a pass that Caster caught behind the Colt defense for an 80-yard touchdown, clinching the game. Namath's total of 496 yards in that game remains the third highest in NFL history. The record of 554 yards was set by Norm Van Brocklin of the Los Angeles Rams in a 1951 game against the New York Yanks, a franchise that later moved to Dallas, where it was nicknamed the Texans, and that eventually emerged as the Baltimore Colts, now the Indianapolis Colts.

Van Brocklin, who later coached the Minnesota Vikings and the Atlanta Falcons, was not blessed with much overall athletic ability.

One opponent once joked that Van Brocklin "runs like a girl with her girdle slipping." Another claimed that "the Dutchman," as Van Brocklin liked to call himself, "couldn't block a baby, couldn't play any other position." But he could play quarterback. He had not only one of the strongest arms in the NFL but also one of the most accurate.

"Go down the right sideline and just keep running," he once told one of his receivers, Tommy McDonald, on the Eagles' 1960 championship team. "I don't know when the ball will hit you, but it will."

It did, for a long touchdown pass. Another time a teammate suggested a contest in practice to test Van Brocklin's accuracy. He asked Van Brocklin to throw a pass about thirty-five yards downfield and let it bounce around until it wobbled to a stop.

"Now what?" Van Brocklin said.

"Now try to hit the ball," the teammate said. "You get ten chances to hit it."

"What if I hit it?" Van Brocklin said.

"If you hit it, I'll buy you a Coke."

With a smile Van Brocklin began aiming passes at the ball in the grass, thirty-five yards downfield. Out of ten passes, he hit the ball six times. He turned to his teammate, who was dumbfounded at his accuracy.

"That's six Cokes," he said.

Then as now, NFL quarterbacks were coached to pass from what coaches called "the pocket," meaning the pocket formed behind the offensive linemen who were blocking the opposing defensive players rushing the passer. Otto Graham and Norm Van Brocklin were two of the best "pocket" passers. So were Johnny Unitas and Joe Namath later on. But by then another type of passer had emerged—the "scrambler."

As the first of the scramblers, Fran Tarkenton developed his style out of necessity. During his first few seasons, which coincided with the Minnesota Vikings' first few seasons, his teammates' blocking often collapsed. As a result he had to run around, or scramble.

In that situation Tarkenton occasionally would tuck the ball under his arm as if he were a halfback and rush for yardage, usually along the sideline. But most of the time he kept running around until he could find an open receiver. At first his scrambling annoyed his coach, who was none other than Norm Van Brocklin, one of the famous pocket passers.

"Stay in the pocket, Francis," the Viking coach would tell him. "The only time a quarterback should run is from terror."

Fran Tarkenton scrambles for a touchdown against the Bears in 1973.

Considering how ineffective some of the Viking pass blockers were, terror often developed. Van Brocklin understood that. In the Vikings' first year, he once told Tarkenton that "those Bears will be coming at you Sunday like you were a piece of chocolate cake." To preserve himself, Tarkenton scrambled. He was so successful at it that as the Vikings improved into a contender, he improved his technique as a scrambler.

"We'd like Francis to throw more out of the pocket," Van Brocklin eventually said, "but Francis has this ability to scramble around. It's a plus."

In his eighteen seasons, including five as the New York Giants' quarterback, Tarkenton completed a record 3,686 passes for a record 47,003 yards and a record 342 touchdowns. His success created a new breed of quarterbacks who scrambled almost by design. In the coaches' language, they were "roll-out" passers, who moved toward the sideline before passing rather than dropping straight back into the "pocket" of blockers. Coach Hank Stram used that roll-out style for Len Dawson when the Kansas City Chiefs won Super Bowl IV.

As coaches gradually accepted the concept of scrambling, Roger Staubach of the Dallas Cowboys emerged as an escape artist who either darted away from pass rushers before throwing or scooted upfield for rushing yardage.

Slender and quick on his feet, Staubach was at his best in the last few minutes of a close game with the outcome at stake. Against the Redskins he once ran 29 yards for the winning touchdown in the final minutes. In a 1972 playoff game against the 49ers, he fired two touchdown passes in the last two minutes for a stunning 30–28 victory. Although the Cowboys' coach, Tom

Landry, would have preferred that Staubach not scramble, he didn't object.

"Roger does what he must do," Landry once said, "and he does it well. We have no plays where Roger is supposed to run. He runs enough."

In one sense Staubach apparently ran too much. During what would be his final season in 1979, he suffered five concussions in collisions with tacklers. Those concussions contributed to his decision a few months later to end his career. The threat of injury was one reason coaches don't like their quarterbacks to scramble; it exposes them as an unprotected target for tacklers.

Looking to his own future, Staubach wisely called the right play: Don't risk serious injury.

Staubach always was smart. Equally important for a quarterback, he also was a leader. Even though Landry called all the Cowboy plays from the sideline, Staubach had the privilege of changing the play to one he thought might be better. Often he did that when he walked up behind the center and checked the opposing team's defense. In barking signals he would call out words and numbers for the new play he wanted. Changing a play that way is known as using an "audible," something all quarterbacks do.

"Roger can always change the play," Landry often joked, "as long as his play works."

Staubach's play usually did work. One reason for that was the way he barked his "audible," boldly and confidently. As the leader of the offensive unit, a quarterback must make his teammates believe in him as a play caller and as a passer. In some cases that belief begins in the huddle. One of the best quarterbacks in the huddle was Bobby Layne, who led the Detroit Lions to three NFL titles. In the 1953 championship game, the Lions were losing, 16–10, to the Cleveland Browns with about four minutes remaining. With the ball on their own 20-yard line following the kickoff, the Lions leaned into the huddle.

"Just block a little bit," Layne told his teammates, "and ol' Bobby will pass you right to the championship."

He did just that, connecting with wide receiver Jim Doran for a 33-yard touchdown and a 17–16 victory. But every so often a quarterback has to know when to listen to his teammates. During the 1962 season in a game against Washington, the Giants were at the Redskins' 5-yard line. Y.A. Tittle, the Giants' quarterback, already had thrown six touchdown passes. One more and he would tie the NFL record shared by Sid Luckman and Adrian Burk. But in the huddle he called for a running play.

"No, no," said Alex Webster, the Giants' fullback. "Throw a pass."

"I don't want to show 'em up," Tittle said, referring to the Redskins. "We'll run the ball."

"If you don't call a pass," said Frank Gifford, the Giants' halfback, "we're all going to walk off the field."

Tittle surrendered. He threw a pass to tight end Joe Walton for a touchdown, scoring a 49–34 victory.

"You only get a chance like that," Gifford said later, "once in a lifetime."

Tittle also shared with George Blanda the NFL record for touchdown passes in one season, 36, until Dan Marino shattered it in 1984. In only his second year as the Miami Dolphins' quarterback, Marino threw 48 touchdown passes while establishing

Dan Marino threw a record 48 touchdown passes for the Dolphins in 1984.

two other season records with 362 completions and 5,084 passing yards.

"We've never had to tell Dan," said his coach, Don Shula, "that he's too young to do this, or that he's not ready to do that."

Before his third start as a rookie out of the University of Pittsburgh, the tall, husky quarterback was sitting with Shula in Baltimore in the Dolphin locker room. As a hard rain fell outside, Shula pointed to a few plays listed on the game plan.

"We won't use those plays now," the coach said.

"How come?" the rookie quarterback asked.

"It's raining too hard," the coach replied.

"That doesn't make any difference," Marino said.

It didn't. Through continuous rain, Marino completed 11 of 18 passes for 157 yards and two touchdowns in a 21–7 victory. Shula had a quarterback who would impress some of football's most famous passers.

"With a football," Sid Luckman said, "Marino is like William Tell with a bow and arrow."

"For throwing the ball," Joe Namath said, "Marino is the best I've ever seen."

As important as a passer is to every team, a quarterback is dependent on the other members of that team. If a quarterback is surrounded by good players, he has the opportunity to do well. If he's surrounded by lesser players, he won't have much of an opportunity to do well. But by the nature of his being the passer, a quarterback's importance is often out of focus.

Invariably a quarterback will get too much credit when his team wins, too much blame when it loses.

But that's the glory and the price of being a passer, no matter what the level of competition may be.

RECEIVING

"Look the Ball Into Your Hands"

When the Los Angeles Raiders won Super Bowl XVIII, their victory represented that franchise's third championship in a span of eight seasons. During that time almost the entire roster had a turnover in personnel, notably at quarterback and running back. One of the few Raiders to play on all three of those Super Bowl teams was Cliff Branch, a wide receiver whose speed and skills set the strategy of their offense.

"We test the opposing team," said Al Davis, the Raiders' managing general partner who once was the team's coach, "by making them try to cover Cliff."

Judging from Davis's philosophy, Branch was the most strategically important offensive player on those three Super Bowl teams, a tribute to the value of a wide receiver. In those three games he caught a total of 14 passes for 181 yards and 3 touchdowns. But even when opposing teams succeeded in limiting his receptions, usually by using both a cornerback and a safety to cover him, other areas often were vulnerable to other Raider receivers.

"Cliff stretched the field for us," Davis said. "By the other team having to stay with him deep, other things were open—sometimes another pass, sometimes a run."

129

Wide receiver Cliff Branch "stretched the field" for the Raiders.

Just as a football team needs a good passer, it also needs good pass receivers. No matter how accurate a pass is, if it's not caught, it's simply another incompletion.

More than anything else, a receiver needs good hands to hold a pass. If he isn't able to hold a pass, he should look for another position. But other talents are necessary. To be effective, a receiver needs the speed to get downfield past the defensive backs. He needs the moves, or the fakes, to fool defensive backs into believing he is going in one direction when he knows he will actually go in another direction. He needs the strength and courage to fight for the ball "in a crowd," as coaches say, meaning in a tangle with one or perhaps two defensive backs. He needs the ability to escape for extra yardage instead of being tackled immediately. And he needs to work with his passer in developing their timing—the precise moment when he is in the clear and the ball is on its way.

Once upon a time pass receivers were known simply as ends; later they were known as flankers, split ends, and tight ends. Now they are known as wide receivers and tight ends.

The wide receivers line up wide, usually one to the right and one to the left; sometimes they both line up on the same side (either right or left) with the inside man in what is called the slot. When teams use three wide receivers, two usually line up either to the right or to the left. The tight end usually lines up next to the right tackle, occasionally next to the left tackle. Some teams use a double tight end formation, either with one next to each tackle or with the two tight ends side by side.

On running plays the tight end is used to block. For that reason a tight end is usually bigger and stronger than a wide receiver, but not as fast as a wide receiver.

Mike Ditka, later the coach of the Bears, was one of the first tight ends. When he was drafted from the University of Pittsburgh by the Bears, he was thought of primarily as a linebacker. But the Bear coach then, George Halas, preferred to utilize his ability to catch the ball along with his ability to block. Other early tight ends in the evolution of the position were Ron Kramer of the Packers, John Mackey of the Colts, and Pete Retzlaff of the Eagles. In recent years Kellen Winslow of the San Diego Chargers added a new dimension—height and speed. Winslow is 6-5 and weighs 242 pounds.

"When you think about Winslow, you think about Superman," said Don Shula, the Dolphin coach. "He climbs the highest buildings."

Since the passer must know where a receiver will be, a receiver never runs just anywhere he wants to go. Instead he runs what coaches call a pass pattern or a pass route. Each pattern or route is designed for a receiver to run a certain way to a certain area of the field. On a 5-yard square-out pattern, for example, a wide receiver would run exactly 5 yards straight downfield, then cut at a ninety-degree angle to the sideline. On a post pattern, a wide receiver or a tight end would run downfield, then angle toward the goalposts.

When a team needs a first down, a receiver tries to make sure that he is downfield far enough so that a completed pass would provide a first down, not leave his team short of it.

One of the masters of the first-down completion was Fred Biletnikoff, a Raider teammate of Cliff Branch for several seasons. Not as fast as Branch, he used deception to fool the cornerbacks assigned to cover him. He also used dedication, staying to prac-

Wide receiver Lynn Swann of the Steelers dazzled in Super Bowl X.

tice long after the Raiders' team workout was over. He would find someone to throw extra passes, perhaps one of the backup quarterbacks or sometimes an equipment manager. For half an hour, occasionally longer, Biletnikoff would practice his patterns and practice the apparently simple process of catching a pass.

With a defensive back all over him, however, it's not always simple for a receiver to catch a pass.

To assure concentration by a receiver, coaches use a familiar phrase as a constant reminder—"look the ball into your hands"—meaning that a receiver should keep his eyes on the ball until he has grasped it firmly and pulled it into his body. But to be where the passer believes he will be, a receiver must run his pattern as precisely as possible. On most patterns a passer will lead his receiver, meaning he will throw the ball to where the receiver will be when the ball gets there. That helps a receiver keep his body between the defensive back covering him and the ball.

Don Hutson, who holds more pass-receiving records than any other NFL player, is believed to have been the first to understand the advantage of running precise patterns.

Tall at 6-1 but slender at 178 pounds, Hutson joined the Green Bay Packers in 1935 from the University of Alabama, where he had been an All-America selection on his senior team, a Rose Bowl winner. In that last year before the NFL draft of college talent began, Hutson signed with the Packers because they had a respected passer in Arnie Herber at a time when many other NFL teams were using offenses built around running backs. In later years Cecil Isbell succeeded Herber as the Packers' quarterback. In eleven seasons Hutson led the league in scoring five times, in pass receiving eight times, in pass-receiving yardage seven times, and in pass-receiving touchdowns nine times.

As a receiver Hutson scored a record 99 touchdowns—eleven more than Don Maynard, one of Joe Namath's favorite receivers on the Jets, and fourteen more than Lance Alworth, a leaper known as "Bambi" in his best seasons with the Chargers. Hutson also holds the record for most touchdowns by a receiver in one season: 17.

Hutson's startling statistics have endured for forty years, but

Hall of Famer Don Hutson practices "looking the ball" into his hands.

what made him special was his gift of drifting through defensive backfields as if he were a patch of fog. Perhaps his most famous move occurred in a game against the Rams, then based in Cleveland. Hutson sprinted toward the end zone, along with Dante Magnani, the Ram defender covering him. As the Packers' end approached the goalposts, which in those years were planted on the goal line, he grabbed an upright with one arm and spun around the pole. Magnani kept going, looking back in time to see Hutson catch a pass for a touchdown.

Several years later, during the Vince Lombardi era in Green Bay, some Packers got tired of hearing old-timers brag about how good Hutson had been. One day they decided to look at some old films, which quickly convinced them of Hutson's skill.

"He's even better than the old-timers told us he was," said Jesse Whittenton, then a Packer cornerback. "He had moves that some of the receivers around now haven't even thought of yet. Hutson was great."

Perhaps the most unusual praise of Hutson's style came when Willie Mays, the Hall of Fame baseball player, attributed his skill at catching long fly balls near the outfield fence to Hutson.

"I saw Hutson in the movies once," Mays said. "I saw how he caught the ball and stopped real fast. I told myself that if he could do that with a football, I could do it with a baseball. I went out and ran hard at the fence and stopped. I kept doing it until I could do it well. He'd catch the ball and twist away from a guy going to tackle him. I caught a baseball and twisted away from the fence."

In the NFL Hutson raised the stature of the pass receiver, thereby raising the stature of the passing game as a strategic weapon.

Shortly after World War II some teams began using three pass receivers rather than two. The third was technically a halfback, but he lined up so far to the right or left that he was considered to be "flanked" near the sideline—hence the name flankerback or simply flanker (now called a wide receiver). Two of the first flankers were Elroy (Crazy Legs) Hirsch of the Los Angeles Rams and Dub Jones of the Cleveland Browns.

Hirsch and Jones each had been a running back in college and during their first few pro seasons. But in order to take full advantage of their speed as receivers, each was used as a flanker.

With the gradual increase in emphasis on passing, the receiver on the other side of the field from the flanker eventually was "split" out so far from the tackle that he became known as the split end. After a few years the NFL decided not to differentiate between them anymore. From then on, each was simply a wide receiver. According to the latest offensive philosophy, some teams use as many as three wide receivers (plus the tight end), leaving only one running back lined up behind the quarterback.

Although speed was always a factor in choosing pass receivers, many coaches' desire for speed and more speed occurred following the success of Bob Hayes, a former Olympic sprint gold medalist, with the Dallas Cowboys.

At the 1964 Summer Olympics in Tokyo, Hayes won the 100-meter dash and ran the anchor leg for the victorious United States team in the 4 × 100-meter relay. The following year he joined the Cowboys, after having been an outstanding college football player at Florida A & M. Through the years some world-class sprinters, such as Buddy Young, had succeeded in the NFL, but others had not—notably Ray Norton.

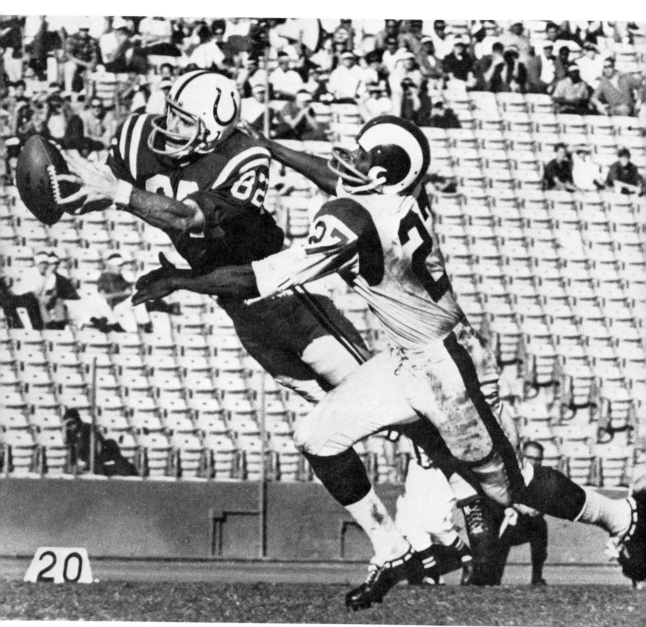

Raymond Berry of the Colts reaches to catch Johnny Unitas' pass.

The difference was that Hayes, like Young, had been a football player who also was a sprinter.

"Bob Hayes was a football player who became an Olympic champion," explained Jake Gaither, his college coach, "not an Olympic champion who tried to be a football player."

But even with his football background, Hayes had difficulty adjusting to NFL collisions.

"I can't get past the linebacker. He grabs me every time," Hayes once told a Cowboy assistant coach during his rookie season. "He won't let me get past him."

"You've got to learn to get past him," the coach said.

"I can't do it," Hayes said. "He gets me every time."

"You'll learn how to do it," the coach said, "or you'll be on your way home."

Hayes learned. So did other football players who happened to be sprinters, such as Cliff Branch. And because they learned, they increased the strategic importance of the wide receiver.

KICKING

"I Lined Up at a Forty-Five-Degree Angle"

When soccer-style kickers, many imported from Europe, began appearing in the NFL during the 1960s, some people laughed— even some teammates of those kickers.

"Our kicker," Alex Karras, a defensive tackle for the Detroit Lions, often joked, "would come on the field yelling, 'I am going to kick a touchdown.'"

Nobody laughs anymore. Almost every NFL team has a soccer-style placekicker now. So do most college and high school teams. Soccer-style kickers are a reminder that the "foot" is still in football. When the sport began more than a century ago, the ball was meant to be kicked, not thrown. Hence the name of the game was football.

On many teams the kicker is smaller and shorter than the other players. It isn't necessary for a kicker to be as tall or as heavy as most other football players. Many of the NFL place-kickers are under 6 feet and weigh about 175 pounds. Placekicking and punting are positions that require mostly leg strength, concentration, and poise.

For all the emphasis on passing and running today, placekicking and punting still represent an important part of football.

Coaches speak of their "special teams." But that is merely another name for their kicking teams—the field-goal/extra-point unit, the kickoff unit, the punting unit. To thwart those units, an opponent also has a unit that tries to block the field goal or the extra point as well as a kickoff-return unit and a punt-return unit.

Each team usually has two specialists. The placekicker tries to make field goals (worth three points) and the point after touch-down (worth one point). He also kicks off. The punter tries to boot the ball deep into the other team's territory, usually on fourth down.

Of the two, the placekicker is in the headlines more often, for better or for worse. Sometimes he will kick a field goal or an extra point that creates the margin of victory in a game. Sometimes he will miss a field goal or an extra point that is the difference in a loss. Hero or goat—that is his glory and his burden.

Although soccer-style placekickers are numerous now, the im-portance of a field-goal kicker was established by Lou (The Toe) Groza of the Cleveland Browns. He was a conventional kicker, meaning that he stood squarely to the goalposts and swung one foot straight ahead, kicking the ball with the square toe of his football shoe.

In contrast, a soccer-style kicker stands at a forty-five-degree angle to where his holder will spot the ball, then strides and swings one leg from the side, kicking it with the side of his foot.

Until Groza came along, most placekickers did not try field goals from beyond the 40-yard line. In 1946, when the Browns were playing in the All-America Football Conference, he was a substitute offensive lineman as well as a kicker. That season Coach Paul Brown noticed that as soon as the Browns' offense neared midfield, Groza would start unlimbering his right leg on the sidelines. One day Brown turned to him.

Lou Groza, who shrunk the field in half as the Browns' field-goal kicker.

"Do you think you can kick one this long?" the coach asked. "I think I can," Groza said. "I'd sure like to try one."

That season Groza kicked a 49-yard field goal and a 50-yard field goal, as well as another 50-yard field goal in Miami against a howling tropical wind. With their powerful placekicker, the Browns had shrunk the field in half. To get a quick three points on a field goal, they had only to move their offense into Groza's range.

In his NFL career, Groza kicked 234 field goals, not counting the 16-yarder that won the 1950 championship game, 28–27, over the Rams. He also developed into an All-NFL offensive tackle.

During that era some placekickers also played another position, as Groza did. George Blanda, a quarterback with the Bears before moving on to the Houston Oilers and the Oakland Raiders, kicked as recently as the 1975 season—when he was forty-eight years old. Blanda established the NFL record for scoring. He accumulated 2,002 total points as he kicked 335 field goals, 943 extra points, and as a quarterback also scored 9 touchdowns.

The one-season NFL record for scoring is held by Paul Hornung, the Packers' halfback and placekicker in 1960 when he produced 176 points—15 field goals, 15 touchdowns, and 41 extra points.

In 1964 the Buffalo Bills signed the first soccer-style placekicker, Pete Gogolak, a rookie out of Cornell University who had been kicking that way for six years. As a junior at the Ogdensburg (New York) Free Academy not far from the St. Lawrence River, he was a tight end on the football team. The day before their first game, Coach Bill Plimpton asked for volunteers to be the placekicker. Gogolak raised his hand. So did two teammates.

"The other two kicked straight ahead," Gogolak has said, "then I lined up at a forty-five-degree angle."

Gogolak had learned to kick a soccer ball in Hungary before his family immigrated to the United States after the Soviet suppression of the revolution there.

"The coach yelled, 'Hey, Gogo, we do it different over here,' and the holder, a quarterback named Steve Munn, looked at me as if he thought I was going to kick him instead of the ball," Gogolak once recalled with a laugh. "But I asked the coach to let me try it my way. When the ball was snapped, I got off a 50-yard kick, but the ball never got higher than three feet off the ground.

"Everybody was yelling, 'Send this guy back to Europe!' but I knew I had something. I didn't kick that year, but I went out on

Pete Gogolak, the first of pro football's soccer-style placekickers.

my own and kicked off a tee. The next year I tried three field goals and made two. I kicked off, mostly. The first time the returners were on the 25-yard line, and I kicked the ball over their heads into the end zone.

"My father sent some of my game films to Syracuse, but the coach then, Ben Schwartzwalder, wasn't interested. My father contacted Cornell, and the freshman coach called back, and that's where I went. But even after I'd kicked well at Cornell, there was almost total unacceptance of the soccer style. None of the NFL teams drafted me that year."

The Bills, then in the AFL, drafted him in the twelfth round after a tryout.

"I had to go up there and kick in the snow for them," Gogolak said. "My first game, an exhibition against the Jets in Tampa, I kicked a 57-yard field goal, the longest one I ever kicked. That year, 1964, we won the AFL title."

Before the 1966 season Gogolak signed with the New York Giants, hastening the NFL-AFL merger.

"That same year my brother Charley joined the Redskins, the next year Jan Stenerud joined the Chiefs, and after that American kids started kicking a football soccer-style, even if they didn't have a European background. Kicking also attracted American kids who were soccer players."

Stenerud came to America from Norway as a skier for Montana State before joining the college football team. Through the 1984 season he held the NFL career record for field goals, with a total of 358, while with the Chiefs, Packers, and Vikings.

By that time the straight-ahead style had virtually vanished in the NFL. One of the few remaining straight-ahead kickers was

Mark Moseley, the only kicker ever chosen as the NFL's most valuable player. He was honored in 1982 when the Redskins went on to win Super Bowl XVII.

"I had a great year," Moseley said at the time, "but a kicker is only as good as his holder and his snapper."

For a placekicker, the snap from the center to the ball holder must be consistently accurate. Most centers study the spiral of their snap, so that the laces on the football will be facing away from the ball holder when he catches it and spots it, holding it gently with a forefinger atop one end. If a kicker were to kick the side where the laces are, it might affect the accuracy of the kick. The ball holder needs good hands to spot the ball quickly. The ball is always spotted 7 yards behind the line of scrimmage for field goals and extra points. According to coaches, that distance enables the placekicker to boot the ball quickly enough as well as high enough on a trajectory above the outstretched hands of the defensive players trying to block it.

"It's a three-man operation," Moseley said, thinking of his center and his holder, "but you always need good blocking, too."

For a punter it's a two-man operation—the punter and his center, also known as a long snapper. On a punt, the punter stands 15 yards behind the line of scrimmage. He needs that distance because he needs more time. He must catch the snap cleanly, step forward, and then follow through, usually with his kicking leg finishing high above his head. Because a punter is unable to protect himself, roughing the punter is a 15-yard penalty—unless the punt is blocked in the process.

Although a good average for a punter is anything over 40 yards, the record punt in the NFL is 98 yards, set by Steve O'Neal of the Jets in 1969 at Denver.

Ray Guy of the Raiders punted the ball into the Superdome's gondola.

With the ball on the Jets' 1-yard line, O'Neal had only 11 yards to work with instead of the usual 15 yards. Waiting for the ball, he was standing inches inside the back line of the end zone. Punting quickly to avoid the Broncos' rush, he boomed the ball high. Perhaps helped by the thin air in Mile High Stadium, the ball soared up and beyond the Bronco punt returner. The ball fell near the 30-yard line, meaning it had traveled nearly 80 yards in the air, then bounced toward the goal line. Hoping that the ball would hop into the end zone for a touchback, thereby putting the ball at their own 20-yard line, the Broncos let it go. But the ball rolled to a stop at the 1-yard line—98 yards from where the play had begun.

"From the 1 to the 1—you can't kick it any farther than that," O'Neal said. "It's a record that can be tied but never broken."

Through the years the record career punting average has endured at 45.10 yards, set by Sammy Baugh, more famous as the Redskins' passer. His average of 51.40 in 1940 is the one-season record. The most respected punter in recent years has been Ray Guy of the Raiders, with a career average of nearly 43 yards. His most memorable punt occurred in the 1976 Pro Bowl at the Louisiana Superdome. A television-screen gondola hung ninety feet above the field.

"Is it all right," Guy asked John Madden, the AFC coach, "if I try to hit the gondola?"

Madden agreed. On his next punt Guy boomed the ball up, up, and into the gondola. Whistles blew. He was ordered to punt again. But more than anything else, Ray Guy, out of Southern Mississippi, has proven how important a kicker can be. In the 1973 draft the Raiders had selected him on the first round.

BLOCKING

"Great Offensive Linemen Are Smart"

In the years when Sammy Baugh was the Redskins' quarterback, he appeared one night as a guest speaker at a meeting in Washington of Federal Bureau of Investigation agents. When he stepped to the microphone, he looked around at all the G-men, as they were known in that era.

"Gentlemen," he said smiling, "this is the most protection I've had all year."

His audience laughed. But to be successful, a passer or a running back must have protection, meaning he must have teammates who block effectively. Of all the skills in football, blocking is one of the most important and also one of the least appreciated. When a quarterback completes a pass or a running back rumbles for a gain, one reason is the skill of the passer or the ball carrier. But another reason is that good blocking enabled the quarterback to stand there against the pass rush and throw the ball, or enabled the running back to get past opponents trying to tackle him.

"You can design the best offensive plays in football," says John Madden, once the Oakland Raiders' coach, "but if your blockers don't do their job, those plays are worthless."

For that reason, Madden believes, as do many other football

149

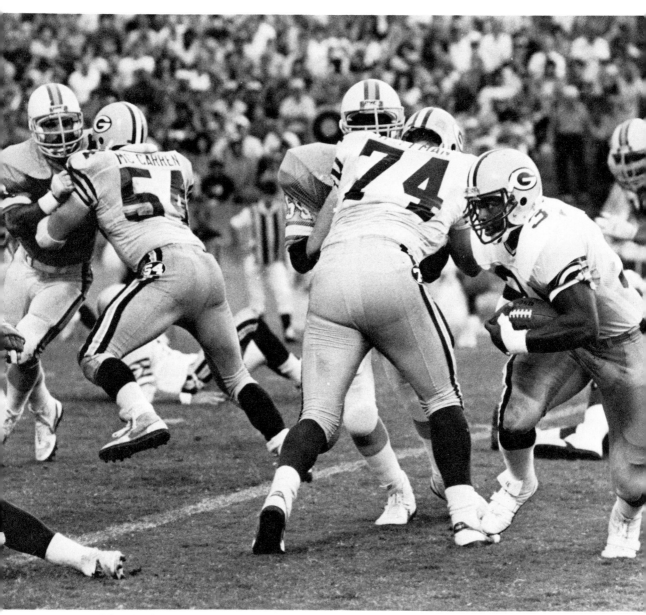

The Packers' offensive line displays textbook blocking for a halfback.

coaches, that in assembling a team the most important single group of players are offensive linemen. Without a good offensive line, a passer doesn't have time to operate with his receivers. Without a good offensive line, a running back is usually tackled before he can go anywhere.

If a team is having a bad season on offense, the fault often can be traced to the offensive line. If a quarterback, for example, is often sacked, which means he's tackled for a loss of yardage before he can pass, his line isn't protecting him. If a running back isn't getting much room to run, his line isn't opening many holes for him.

Turning that theory around, if a team is playing well on offense, it's usually because the offensive line is blocking well.

In today's football the offensive line consists, from left to right, of a tackle, a guard, a center who snaps the ball, a guard, and a tackle. On a running play a tight end is also considered a lineman because he is blocking; some teams use two tight ends. (On a pass play a tight end is usually a receiver.) But on a pass play usually one running back, often the fullback, remains to block for the quarterback in case an opposing linebacker rushes.

By the nature of their role, offensive linemen usually toil without attention, usually without a nickname. Every so often, however, an offensive line becomes popular enough to be dubbed with a nickname. One of the few offensive lines ever to emerge as slightly famous was the "Electric Company," who blocked for O.J. (The Juice) Simpson of the Buffalo Bills in 1973 when he set an NFL one-season rushing record of 2,003 yards.

"They called us the 'Electric Company,'" guard Reggie McKenzie said, "because we turned on the Juice."

Around that same time the Miami Dolphins, repeating as Super Bowl champions, had their "Mushrooms."

"They called us the 'Mushrooms'" guard Bob Kuechenberg said, "because we were kept in the dark."

The Washington Redskins had their "Hogs," who blocked for quarterback Joe Theismann and running back John Riggins when they won Super Bowl XVII, 27–17, over the Miami Dolphins. During the Redskins' success, the Hogs joined Miss Piggy and the Three Little Pigs as the most storied swine in history. In height and weight the Hogs were huge:

> Left Tackle: Joe Jacoby, 6-7, 311.
> Left Guard: Russ Grimm, 6-3, 292.
> Center: Jeff Bostic, 6-2, 258.
> Right Guard: Mark May, 6-6, 295.
> Right Tackle: George Starke, 6-5, 270.

If those five Hogs were prodded into a stockyard, their weight would add up to 1,426 pounds, give or take their latest meal. Their nickname developed one day during training camp in 1982 with Joe Bugel, the Redskin assistant coach in charge of the offensive line, stared at Grimm thoughtfully.

"You," said Bugel, "are a prototype hog."

Hearing that, the Redskin offensive linemen laughed at what they considered a compliment. Soon they were calling themselves the Hogs. To show their admiration for Riggins, the linemen named their fullback an honorary Hog because, as Grimm says, "He's like us—he likes to get down in the mud." To be a good blocker, an offensive lineman must like to get his uniform dirty. To be a good blocker, there is no other way.

Joe Theismann drops back to pass as the "Hogs" protect him.

For an offensive lineman, however, there are two types of blocking—pass blocking and run blocking.

In pass blocking, which means backing up to protect the quarterback as he retreats to search for a receiver, an offensive lineman must be what coaches call a "dancer." He must use small, quick steps to stay between his quarterback and the defensive lineman who is trying to muscle past him. For some offensive linemen, accustomed to blocking mostly on running plays in college, it takes time to adjust to the pass blocking that NFL coaches demand. Every so often an All-America guard is unable to make the NFL because he can't make that adjustment.

In run blocking, which means trying to open a hole in the defense for a running back, an offensive lineman usually relies on what coaches call a "power" or a "drive" block. He comes off the line into the defensive player opposite him and tries to drive that player as far as possible. Depending on the matchup, driving that defensive player two or three yards is considered a good block. Sometimes even a standstill is enough for a running back to scoot past the defender. But if a blocker loses ground, he seldom succeeds.

One of the NFL's best offensive linemen is John Hannah, the 6-3, 270-pound guard of the New England Patriots, a consistent All-Pro.

"John's not just big, he's smart," says Dick Steinberg, the Patriots' director of personnel development. "You'll find that great offensive linemen are smart people."

For some reason offensive linemen often are misrepresented as big, strong blobs who aren't smart enough to play any other position.

As proof that this isn't so, consider that in 1968, when Paul Brown took command of the Cincinnati Bengals as an expansion team, the first player he drafted was not a quarterback or a running back or a pass receiver or a linebacker. The first player was Bob Johnson, a center from the University of Tennessee.

"With this young man," Brown said, "we have a player who will anchor our offensive line for the next decade."

Johnson played twelve seasons, helping the Bengals develop into a consistent contender. Some coaches consider the center, aside from the quarterback, to be the most important player on the offensive unit. One of the most famous centers, Chuck Bed-

John Riggins takes handoff as the "Hogs" keep the Ram tacklers at bay.

When a block is missed, John Riggins faces the consequences.

narik of the Philadelphia Eagles, was also a linebacker. When the NFL adopted two-platoon football in 1950, virtually every player concentrated on his role on either the offensive unit or the defensive unit. Although Bednarik was primarily a linebacker, occasionally he would fill in at center—two positions he had played as an All-American at Penn.

For the 1960 season the Eagles decided to use Bednarik at center in order to ease his physical burden as much as possible. But when their supply of linebackers was reduced by injuries, Coach Buck Shaw asked him to finish a game at outside linebacker while remaining at center on offense.

As it turned out, Bednarik finished the season both as a linebacker on defense and as a center on offense. The only time he was off the field was during kickoffs, punts, and placekicks. When the Eagles defeated the Packers, 17–13, for the NFL championship that year, Bednarik not only played a total of fifty-eight minutes, but he also made the tackle on Jim Taylor in the final play that preserved the title. As he sat on top of the Packer fullback, the gun went off, ending the game.

"All right, Jimmy," he said, "you can get up now. The game's over."

Some of football's most legendary players have been offensive linemen. The 49ers once had an offensive tackle, Bob St. Clair, who ate raw meat. Not rare, raw. In a restaurant he once looked at the menu and then looked up at the waiter.

"I'll have the steak," he said. "Raw."

"Did you say rare, sir?" the waiter asked. "Did you say you want your steak rare?"

"No, I want it raw."

"Raw?" the waiter said.

"That's right," St. Clair said. "Take it out of the refrigerator and put it on a plate."

"Yes, sir," the waiter said.

Another offensive tackle, Bob Brown, a 290-pounder who played mostly for the Eagles before finishing his NFL career with the Rams and the Raiders, had powerful arms. The day he joined the Raiders at their training camp, he walked by himself to the goalposts at the far end of the practice field. Getting down into his stance, the man known as the Boomer rammed his taped right forearm into one of the uprights. After wobbling for a moment, the upright toppled backward, tilting the crossbar askew.

"He actually knocked down the goalpost," John Madden recalls.

Imagine what the Boomer did to humans he had to block. That's one reason so many coaches believe that their most important players are offensive lineman.

TACKLING

"DEE-fense, DEE-fense"

Almost from the moment Lawrence Taylor joined the New York Giants as a rookie in 1981, he has been hailed by some observers as the NFL's best player. "No other player," says John Madden, the television football analyst who once was the Oakland Raiders' coach, "can dominate a game single-handedly the way Taylor does." But significantly Taylor is not a quarterback or a running back or a pass receiver. Taylor is a defensive player, an outside linebacker.

Taylor's stature shows how important and how appreciated defense has become in all of football, among college and high school teams as well as NFL teams.

Until 1950, when the NFL changed its rules to permit free substitution, a player was expected to play both ways—offense and defense. A quarterback usually was also a defensive back, a fullback was also a linebacker. But with free substitution, coaches began developing separate units for offense and defense as well as specialists, such as placekickers and punters. As it turned out, some players were better suited, either through ability or temperament, for defense. Those who thrived on the physical aspect of football usually enjoyed defense more.

Soon those players on the defensive unit had their own following. Whenever a home team is ahead now late in a close game and the opposing team gets the ball, the chant of "DEE-fense, DEE-fense" is heard, with the accent on the first syllable.

The word of course is "defense." It is properly pronounced "de-FENSE," with the accent on the second syllable, and the first syllable is properly pronounced "dee," as in "deliver." But now many people pronounce it DEE-fense, the way the New York Giants' fans first did around the time of the team's 1956 NFL championship.

That year the Giants had a defensive unit that included two future Hall of Famers, Andy Robustelli at right end and Sam Huff at middle linebacker.

In previous years one of football's most popular cheers had been "Hold that line," but in beseeching their team to stop the opponent, Giant fans simplified it to "DEE-fense, DEE-fense." Hearing it on television, football fans in other NFL cities and in college stadiums began to use that cheer. So did fans of other sports, notably basketball.

Although DEE-fense is not the preferred pronounciation, when chanted at a sports event, especially a football game, somehow it sounds better.

The cheer also helped to identify the value of the defensive unit. According to coaches at all levels of football, a team won't be successful without a good defense. A team can't hope to outscore its opponents all the time. It must be able to *stop* its opponent from scoring.

In football a defensive unit has four groups of players—linemen, linebackers, cornerbacks, and safeties.

Mark Gastineau of the Jets sacks Bills' quarterback Joe Ferguson.

In a four-man defensive line, there are two ends and two tackles. In a three-man defensive line, there are two ends and what is called a nose tackle because he usually crouches across from the nose of the offensive center who is about to snap the ball to the quarterback. With either four or three players, the defensive line is primarily responsible for the pass rush on the opposing quarterback.

The defensive line is also responsible for stopping running plays, but its ends in particular should be good pass rushers.

Through the years some of the NFL's most popular players have been those on a defensive line—the Steel Curtain of the four-time Super Bowl champion Steelers (L. C. Greenwood, Joe Greene, Ernie Holmes, Dwight White); the Fearsome Foursome of the Rams (Deacon Jones, Merlin Olsen, Roosevelt Grier, Lamar Lundy); the Purple People Eaters of the Vikings (Carl Eller, Alan Page, Gary Larsen, Jim Marshall); the Doomsday Defense of the Cowboys (George Andrie, Jethro Pugh, Bob Lilly, Larry Cole); and the New York Sack Exchange of the Jets (Mark Gastineau, Abdul Salaam, Marty Lyons, Joe Klecko).

Defensive ends usually are taller and quicker than defensive tackles, but not much. The taller the pass rushers are, the harder it is for a quarterback to see over them or through them in trying to find a pass receiver.

For that reason tall quarterbacks are preferred by most coaches. But one of football's most spectacular quarterbacks, Doug Flutie of the New Jersey Generals, who was the 1984 Heisman Trophy winner while at Boston College, is only 5-9¾.

As big as defensive linemen are, they also must be quick, meaning they must be able to move with agility despite their weight. Years ago it was enough for some defensive linemen to be heavy. But with offensive players so much quicker now, the defensive lineman must be even quicker if he is to get around them.

Quickness afoot is not to be confused with speed afoot. Even though a lineman might not be as fast in a 40-yard dash as other players, he might be quicker in darting one way or another for a few steps.

One of the quickest defensive ends was Gino Marchetti, who played on the Colt teams that won the 1958 and 1959 NFL championships. At practice one day Marchetti lined up against a rookie offensive tackle who was unable to cope with the All-Pro's moves. On one play Marchetti faked the rookie to the right, then sped past him on the left. Noticing that the rookie appeared discouraged, Coach Weeb Ewbank had a suggestion.

"Get lower," Ewbank said. "You've got to get your rear end lower if you expect to block Gino."

On the next play the rookie offensive tackle crouched lower. Marchetti faked him to the left this time and went by him on the right. Ewbank shook his head.

"Lower, lower," the coach said, "you've got to get lower."

On the next play the rookie offensive tackle was down even lower. Instead of trying to go around him, Marchetti put one of his hands on the rookie's helmet and leapfrogged *over* him. Startled and frustrated, the rookie looked around at Ewbank.

"What do I do now, coach?" he asked.

"Applaud," Ewbank said with a shrug.

Marchetti was 6-4 and 245 pounds, yet he was able to leapfrog over that husky offensive tackle as if the rookie were a fireplug. That's quickness. That's what offensive tackles must cope with in their man-to-man matchups with defensive ends. Offensive guards, meanwhile, match up with defensive tackles. One of the best defensive tackles was Bob Lilly, a member of the Cowboys' Doomsday Defense.

"Lilly," the Cowboys' coach, Tom Landry, has said, "is the best player I've ever coached."

As a rookie Lilly was used at defensive end, but he floundered at that position. Switched to defensive tackle by Landry, he went on to a Hall of Fame career that included the Cowboys' victory in Super Bowl VI. Years later Landry explained why the 6-5, 225-pound Lilly was more suited to tackle than end.

"At tackle," the Cowboys' coach said, "Bob could be out of position and still get back to make the play because of his great quickness, his agility, his balance, and his strength. At end he didn't have as much time to do that effectively."

Stories of Lilly's strength began at Texas Christian University, where he was known as the "Purple Cloud," after the color of the school's uniform. One day he was with a classmate who teased him about his strength and pointed to a Volkswagen that was parked nearby.

"If you're so strong," his classmate said, "let's see you lift that VW onto the sidewalk."

After walking around the little car to size it up, Lilly lifted the rear end onto the sidewalk. Then he walked around to the front end and lifted that onto the sidewalk. His classmate shook his head in disbelief. Afterward the story of Lilly's strength was exaggerated day by day.

"It got so," Lilly said later, "that some people were saying that I put the car up on the library steps. I'd have needed a crane to do that."

Lilly thrived in the four-three defense that Landry perfected

Bob Lilly of the Cowboys (74) chases Giants' quarterback Y.A. Tittle.

with the Cowboys—four defensive linemen and three linebackers behind them. In recent years some NFL teams have preferred to use a three-four defense: three linemen and four linebackers. Whatever the defense, linebackers provide a triple threat. They must be able to rush the passer in what is called a "blitz." They must be able to stack up a running play up the middle or swoop out near the sideline on a sweep. They must also be able to stay with a swift running back moving out on a pass pattern.

To do this well, a linebacker often must rely on his intuition, an educated guess as to the opposing team's play. Lawrence Taylor is considered to be one of the most intuitive linebackers.

"When the ball is snapped," the Giant linebacker has said, "I can kind of read everything up and down the line. It's an instinct that tells me where to go. I don't know how that is, but it is."

That's intuition, a sense of knowing what to do and how to do it. At 6-3 and 245 pounds, Taylor has that intuition. Since he plays in a three-four defense that uses four linebackers, he is one of two outside linebackers—one outside the right end, the other outside the left end. Between them are the two inside linebackers. But when a team prepares to play the Giants, its coaches are mostly concerned with how to prevent Taylor from disrupting its offense.

"Taylor," said Dick Vermeil, once the Philadelphia Eagles' coach, "can cause you more problems in the preparation of an offensive game plan than any other single player I ever coached against."

In a four-three defense, one middle linebacker is between two outside linebackers. Because he is able to roam wherever the play goes, the middle linebacker has been one of the most popular de-

Sam Huff, a symbol of the start of the era of the middle linebacker.

fensive players. The era of the middle linebacker began when Sam Huff was on the Giants' teams that inspired the "DEE-fense" cheer. "Huff, Huff, Huff!" the Giants' fans would yell, making a sound like that of a locomotive puffing. "Huff, Huff, Huff!" But he was only one of several outstanding NFL middle linebackers then. The others were Ray Nitschke of the Packers, Joe Schmidt of the Detroit Lions, and Bill George of the Bears.

As effective as those four were, Dick Butkus was even better. Joining the Bears in 1965 out of the University of Illinois, he quickly established himself as an All-Pro middle linebacker. By 1970, when O. J. Simpson played against the Bears for the first time, Butkus had a reputation not only for being a hard tackler but for being everywhere on the field.

"As I ran the ball," Simpson said later, "I found myself wondering, 'Where's Butkus, where is he?' "

That's the effect Butkus, at 6-3 and 245 pounds, had on opposing players, especially running backs. Butkus didn't just try to tackle a ball carrier, he tried to make him fumble. He often succeeded. During his senior season at Illinois, he caused 10 fumbles, an extraordinary number.

"I want to get a good measure on a guy and strip him down," he once said. "If I can strip him down and make him drop the ball, that takes it out of guys."

The son of Lithuanian immigrant parents, Butkus had grown up in Chicago with four older brothers, all of whom had played football but not as well as he would. Of the five brothers, however, Dick was the smallest.

Bear linebacker
Dick Butkus had
O.J. Simpson
wondering:
"Where is he?"

"I'm nothing but little brother," he once said. "When they surround me, you can't even see the top of my head. They hide me completely."

But nobody hid Dick Butkus on a football field until knee injuries shortened his career. Unwisely he kept playing on those bad knees until he was unable to run properly. Just about the time he had to stop playing, another middle linebacker arrived who would be compared to him—Jack Lambert of the Steelers.

As a rookie, Lambert took over at middle linebacker on the Steeler team that would win Super Bowl IX. The following season, as the Steelers repeated in Super Bowl X, all three of their linebackers were selected to the All-Pro team—Jack Ham and Andy Russell in addition to Lambert.

"I think that's what I'm proudest of," Lambert once said. "Imagine having all three of our linebackers selected as the NFL's three best linebackers—that's really a great honor. That never happened before. And who knows, it might never happen again. When all three make All-Pro like that, it means that each of us is doing a good job."

At 6-4 and 220 pounds, Lambert often was teased by his teammates for his aggressive style.

"Jack Lambert is so mean," defensive tackle Joe Greene often joked, "he doesn't even like himself."

But in serious moments Greene praised Lambert as the "spark" of the Steeler defense.

For all the headlines about linebackers and defensive linemen, Al Davis, who built the Raider organization into one of the NFL's best, believes that cornerbacks are the most important players on a football team. Not just on defense, but on the *entire* team.

"You start with cornerbacks," Davis says, "and then you build the rest of your team."

When the Los Angeles Raiders won Super Bowl XVIII in January 1984, they had what many football people considered to be the two best cornerbacks on any one team—Lester Hayes at left cornerback and Mike Haynes at right cornerback. The position of cornerback was established in 1952 by Dick (Night Train) Lane, who had played one season at Scottsbluff (Nebraska) Junior College and four seasons with the Fort Ord (California) team—as an offensive end. Discharged from the Army in 1952, he walked into the Los Angeles Rams' office. That year the Rams were the defending NFL champions, but they signed him as a free agent for a $4,500 salary—if he made the team.

Used as an offensive end at first, he was confused by the unfamiliar terminology. Switched to defense, he found himself covering pass receivers as no one else ever had.

As a rookie Lane had 14 interceptions, which is still the NFL record for one season. He also led the NFL in 1954 with 10 interceptions. In his career with the Rams, the Chicago Cardinals, and the Lions, he had 68 interceptions, the most of any cornerback. Two safeties have had more—Paul Krause of the Vikings with 81 and Emlen Tunnell of the Giants and Packers with 79.

"At cornerback," Lane often said, "you're going to get beat, but you've got to have a sense of recovery."

Night Train got his marvelous nickname as a rookie. During his trial as an offensive end in the Rams' training camp, he often visited Tom Fears, the Rams' best receiver, in his dormitory room to talk about pass patterns. Fears had a favorite musical recording, Buddy Morrow's rendition of "Night Train," which he often played on his phonograph. Whenever another rookie, Ben Sheets, stopped by Fears's room, Lane was usually there with "Night Train" playing in the background.

"Hey," said Sheets one day, "there's Night Train."

The name stuck. In the years that followed it sometimes was shortened to Train by teammates and opponents alike. He was so feared as a cornerback that Vince Lombardi, the Packers' coach, once ordered quarterback Bart Starr not to throw a pass in his area.

"Don't throw anywhere near him," Lombardi said. "Train's the best there is."

The responsibilities of a left cornerback and a right cornerback are virtually the same—cover the wide receiver lined up on that side of the field. But the responsibilities of the two safetymen are much different. One is known as the strong safety because he lines up across from the "strong" side of the offensive team, the side with the tight end. On passing plays the strong safety is usually assigned to cover the tight end. The free safety meanwhile is exactly that—free, at least in man-to-man coverage, to roam wherever he thinks he should be, perhaps to join a teammate in double-covering a certain receiver. But in zone coverage, he is assigned to protect a certain area.

The free safety is also available for one of the most exciting plays on defense—the safety blitz.

From about five or six yards behind the line of scrimmage, the free safety shoots past the offensive linemen as if he were a linebacker trying to sack the quarterback. When successful, this is a sensational maneuver. But every so often the free safety is stopped, usually by a husky running back assigned to remain as a blocker for the passer. Larry Wilson, who was a free safety with the St. Louis Cardinals, is credited with inventing the safety blitz.

"It takes the soul of a linebacker," he often said with a smile, "and the mentality of a mule."

Wilson tried to time his blitz so that it coincided with the snap, making it more difficult for a blocker to stop him. When he timed it perfectly, he appeared to pounce on the quarterback as if he were a mountain lion leaping out of a tree.

"The first time I ever did it was against Charlie Conerly of the Giants," he recalled. "He didn't know where I came from."

Wilson was considered one of the NFL's toughest players. Not that big at 6-0 and 190 pounds, he had the eyes of a hawk under a shock of blond hair. His firm jaw symbolized his determination. He once actually played a game in 1965 with both hands in casts. From a distance he appeared to be wearing two white boxing gloves. He not only played, but he also intercepted a pass and returned it 34 yards for a touchdown in a 21–17 victory over the Steelers.

"Larry's not a 'holler' guy," one of his teammates, Jerry Stovall, once said. "Larry's a 'do' guy."

With today's more complicated pass defenses, most NFL coaches use five, six, and even seven defensive backs in certain obvious passing situations. In order to make room for another defensive back, a linebacker usually is removed. Defense has come a long way since the Giants' defensive unit in 1956 was the first in the NFL to be introduced before a game over the public-address system. Ever since then offensive players have had to share the headlines with defensive players.

"Championships," Vince Lombardi once said, "are won on defense."

STRATEGY

Coaching Is Teaching

After a rare disappointing performance by his Notre Dame team, Frank Leahy called his players together for a meeting when they returned to practice on Monday.

"Gentlemen," the famous coach said, holding a football, "we are going back to fundamentals. This object is a football."

Among the players sitting at their lockers, Ziggy Czarobski, an All-America tackle whose wit was as quick as his footwork, raised a hand.

"Not so fast, coach," he said.

Leahy laughed along with all the other Notre Dame players. But that moment contained as much truth as humor in defining what a football coach does.

"They call it coaching," Vince Lombardi once said, "but it is teaching."

That is true in any sport, but even more so in football. When each offensive play begins, all eleven players must move into action together, not separately. On defense all eleven players must react together, not separately. To do that properly and repeatedly, the players must be taught properly and repeatedly. And they must practice it properly and repeatedly under the coach's supervision.

172

At training camp, the blocking sled is among a coach's best friends.

"You do not tell them it is so," Lombardi added. "You show them the reason why it is so, and then you repeat and repeat until they are convinced, until they know."

In football, a coach's first responsibility is teaching the fundamentals to players, especially to youngsters. But even in the NFL some players need to be reminded of various fundamentals, such as footwork and technique, depending on their position on the team. Footwork and technique for a running back, for example, are much different than they are for a defensive tackle. That's one reason why NFL teams, college teams, and even some high school teams have several assistant coaches—to teach players at different positions.

In addition to the head coach, an NFL or a major college team usually has a coach tutoring the quarterbacks, another working with the running backs, another with the pass receivers, another with the offensive linemen, another with the defensive linemen, another with the linebackers, and another with the defensive backs. Most teams also have an offensive coordinator and a defensive coordinator to tie everything together, along with another assistant coach who supervises the "special" teams.

The head coach, of course, makes the final decisions on which players make the starting team as well as the team roster. Selecting the players is not as easy as it sounds. Johnny Unitas, the quarterback who had a Hall of Fame career with the Baltimore Colts, originally was drafted by the Pittsburgh Steelers, who cut him as a rookie at training camp. At the time the Steelers had three other quarterbacks—Jim Finks, Ted Marchibroda, and a rookie, Vic Eaton.

In the NFL, rookies are drafted after the teams have scouted college players at games, on films, and sometimes at individual workouts. In the draft, each team is allowed twelve selections each year; the team with the worst record during the previous season is the first to draft, the next worst team is second, and so on down to the Super Bowl champion, which is the last or twenty-eighth team to draft. Each team usually has more or fewer than twelve choices because they are allowed to trade a choice, even in the first round, to another team.

After the draft is completed, an eligible player who has not been chosen is considered a free agent, meaning he may sign with any of the twenty-eight teams. Some teams, such as the Cowboys, usually sign several dozen free agents; other teams sign only a few. But sometimes a free agent turns out to be an exceptional player. Everson Walls, the Cowboys' cornerback, arrived at their training camp in 1981 as a free agent out of Grambling, where he had led the nation's college players with 11 interceptions. The moment he arrived, his talent was spotted by Tom Landry and the other Cowboy coaches. As a rookie Walls led the NFL with 11 interceptions and was chosen as All-Pro cornerback.

Considering how extensively the NFL teams scout college players, it's hard to understand how Walls was not drafted through twelve rounds, a total of 336 players.

In addition to recognizing talent, a coach also must decide a player's best position. Some psychological studies point out that a player with an aggressive personality is more likely to succeed on defense. It's important for a coach to try to place a player at a position that fits his personality. A coach always tries to find a quarterback with the personality of a leader. But a team needs more than one leader.

"You need leaders everywhere," John Madden, the former Raiders' coach, has said. "On offense, on defense, and on special teams."

In recent years under Tom Flores, as under Madden, the Raiders have been one of the few NFL teams that have continued to let the quarterback call his own plays. On most other teams the coaches call the next play from the sideline, either by sending in a substitute who will inform the quarterback of the play or by an assistant coach wig-wagging signals to the quarterback, similar to those in baseball from a third-base coach to a batter. Paul Brown, believed to be the first coach to send in plays, did it with what were known as "messenger" guards. One of those guards was Chuck Noll, later the Steelers' coach.

John Madden: "You need leaders everywhere."

Then as now, most quarterbacks resent having plays sent in to them. They prefer to call their own plays. As much as Otto Graham, the quarterback on those famous Cleveland teams, respected Paul Brown, he disagreed with his coach's philosophy in this regard.

"We have eleven coaches on the field," Graham once said. "Various players will report to me on plays that might work. Paul Brown also got that information, but my criticism is that he might be one or two plays behind what I would have called."

As with quarterbacks now, Graham had the option of calling a different play if he thought the play that had been sent in would not work. Usually such a change is made at the line of scrimmage in what is known as an audible: the quarterback barks new signals, usually a combination of colors and numbers. To do that well, the quarterback must be a quick thinker; his teammates also must recognize the new signals instantly.

During the 1983 season, Danny White of the Cowboys changed the play during an important game with the Redskins after he discussed the original play with Coach Tom Landry during a time-out. Watching from the sideline, Landry could be seen yelling, "No, no," in an unusual display of annoyance. White's play didn't succeed.

Landry had several reasons for preferring to send in plays to his quarterback, as do all the coaches who prefer this method. First, the coach feels he has a better knowledge of which play will work best in that situation. Second, by knowing what the play is going to be, he is better able to watch how it develops. Third, by using a certain play at a certain time, he feels he might be able to set up the use of another play later in the game. Fourth, he is constantly

Tom Landry discusses strategy with Roger Staubach and Mike Ditka.

being alerted to developments in the opposing team's defense by assistant coaches perched in a booth on the press-box level.

But the argument continues—who knows better?

Norm Van Brocklin, the Hall of Fame quarterback with the Rams and Eagles who later coached the Vikings and the Falcons, believed that the quarterback knew better. He let his quarterbacks call the plays.

"You give a quarterback a ready list and feed him information," Van Brocklin said. "But he's the only one who can get the actual feel of the play on the field. The quarterback has to be the leader."

Another decision for a head coach, of course, occurs every time his offense is faced with fourth down.

In order to gain another first down, his team must advance the ball at least ten yards from where it began on first down. But if his team is close to a first down, say one yard or less, a coach has to decide whether to try to run or pass for at least the necessary yardage. If his team is close to a first down but within the range of his placekicker, a coach must decide whether to continue the drive for a touchdown or be content with a field goal attempt. And in almost any other situation on fourth down, he must decide whether it is better to punt.

No matter what the coach decides, if his decision doesn't work out to his team's advantage, he will be second-guessed by his team's fans for having made the wrong decision.

Anybody can second-guess a coach *after* the play is over or *after* the game is over. But the coach has only one guess—what will work best in this particular situation at this particular time. If the play of his choice turns out to be successful, especially if it wins the game, he is hailed as a genius. But if the play backfires, he is criticized for having made a mistake. For the fan it's fun to second-guess the coach for a mistake. But the coach also deserves credit when he makes a decision that is successful.

Just as a coach makes mistakes in judgment, players make mistakes in executing their plays.

Win or lose, coaches often say that "football is a game of mistakes," meaning that the team with the fewest mistakes usually wins. Quite often a player's mistake will result in a penalty—illegal motion by a running back, holding by an offensive lineman, defensive pass interference by a cornerback, to name only three. In recent years one of the NFL's least-penalized teams has been the Miami Dolphins, coached by Don Shula.

"You just don't make mistakes when you play for Shula—he

won't stand for it," fullback Larry Csonka once said. "If you do, you're gone."

Instilling that determination in his players not to make mistakes is part of how a good coach motivates his team. His players concentrate on their assignments, no matter what position each plays. They don't jump offside. They don't forget to stay with a certain pass receiver. Above all they don't forget the offensive play or the defensive coverage. Throughout football history that has been the trademark of the best teams and the best coaches.

In motivating players with words, the best coaches have all been a little different.

Some have been dramatic, as Knute Rockne was when he told his Notre Dame team to "win one for the Gipper." Others have been emotional, as Vince Lombardi was when he told his Packers before the first Super Bowl, "You're representing the entire National Football League." Others have been scientific, as Tom Landry was in explaining the Cowboys' game plan. Others have been sentimental, as Bear Bryant was when he told his Alabama players that they had "good mamas and papas."

Year after year the best coaches seem to have the best teams—not always championship teams, but usually winning teams.

Such success prompts a question—do the best coaches attract the best players, or do the best coaches make the players they have play better than other coaches could? The answer is a little of both. In college football, where a player has a choice of what school he wants to attend, a famous coach will attract more good players than a lesser-known coach will.

"I went to Alabama," said Ray Perkins, once a Crimson Tide wide receiver and later their coach, "because I wanted to play for Bear Bryant."

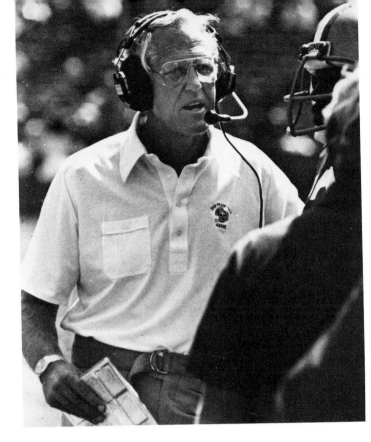

Bill Walsh
discusses strategy
with his 49er
aides perched
upstairs.

Through the years other players have gone to Notre Dame, Oklahoma, Southern Cal, Grambling, and dozens of other famous football colleges to play for certain coaches. But in the NFL a player (unless he is a free agent) doesn't have a choice of teams. He must report to the team that selected him in the draft of college players. Even so, the same coaches keep producing some of the best teams—Don Shula with the Colts and the Dolphins, Chuck Noll with the Steelers, Tom Landry with the Cowboys, Bill Walsh with the 49ers, Bud Grant with the Vikings. Chuck Knox has coached the Rams, the Bills, and the Seattle Seahawks into the playoffs.

Obviously these coaches lift the skill level of their players, no matter what the turnover of the roster.

Because football is more of an emotional game than, say, baseball, the football coach seems to be more important to a team's success than a baseball manager is. One reason for the emotional character of football is that it is played only once a week. Through several days of practice, a team builds to a peak for that game. In contrast baseball is played almost every day on the major league level. With that daily schedule, emotional peaks and valleys would wear out a player. But in football, players seem to react to emotion.

"Without emotion it's hard to win a football game," Tom Landry has said. "If the other team has emotion and your team doesn't, chances are the other team is going to win."

For all the coaching and emotions involved, of course, a team still needs good players to win, usually better ones than the opposing team has. Without such players a good coach is helpless. He may make his men perform somewhat better than they otherwise would. But that doesn't mean he can make a team of poor players capable of beating a team with much better players. Perhaps that was never more clearly shown then in the years when Johnny Lattner, a Notre Dame halfback who later won the 1953 Heisman Trophy, was the best player on Frank Leahy's team. One day Leahy's wife Floss broke her leg in a household accident. At the hospital she phoned her husband during the second day of practice.

"Frank," she said, "I'm sorry to call you off the practice field, but I'm in the hospital."

"What's wrong, Floss?"

"I broke my left leg."

"Are you all right?" the coach asked.

"I'm all right."

In one of his last NFL games, Y.A. Tittle suffers the agony of a sack.

The coach's wife paused, then said, "Frank?"

"Yes, Floss, what is it?"

"Better me than Johnny Lattner, huh, Frank?"

Yes, good coaches need good players. But without good coaches, good players don't always perform up to their potential. Despite the sometimes complicated vocabulary of football, it remains a game that depends on two basic elements—blocking on offense, tackling on defense. For all the mystique that surrounded his coaching, Vince Lombardi never pretended to confuse the issue.

"This game," he often said, "is blocking and tackling. If you do that better than the other team does, you win."

As with all outstanding coaches, Vince Lombardi also believed in the discipline that creates effective blocking and tackling, the discipline that helps a team avoid costly mistakes. That discipline, he knew, begins with the coach.

"The perfect name for the perfect coach," he once said, "would be Simple Simon Legree."

WHY IS FOOTBALL SO POPULAR?

For several years now, football has rivaled baseball as America's most popular sport.

One reason is that television, with its instant replays, has provided another look at action that often happened too fast to be fully appreciated by the spectators in the stadium. But perhaps the most important reason is that football is rooted in America on four levels—from neighborhood leagues for youngsters up through high schools and colleges and on to the National Football League.

Just about everybody can root for a team at one of those competitive levels, if not for teams on several levels.

Part of football's appeal is that it's a physical game. It's known as a contact sport, but Vince Lombardi once defined football properly. "Dancing is a contact sport," he said. "Football is a collision sport." In football, a collision sometimes produces an injury. That's why the players wear so much protective equipment, such as helmets and shoulder pads. But the collisions are what a real football player enjoys. The collisions are also what a real football fan enjoys.

Unlike most other sports, football is basically played by a team

185

With his feet as quick as his arm, Joe Montana scores in Super Bowl XIX.

only once a week. As a result a football game is more of an event for its fans than baseball, basketball, or ice hockey, the other major spectator sports.

For many of those fans interested in college football or the NFL or both, television provides that event. Several college games are usually televised on a Saturday, two and occasionally three NFL games on a Sunday, with another NFL game broadcast on a Monday night. For three years, beginning in 1983, the United States Football League enabled fans to watch games during the spring and summer until they switched to a fall schedule.

More than most sports, football is subject to the second-guess by any fan worth the mustard on a hot dog.

Anytime a play doesn't work, the fan in the stands or watching television will wonder why a different play wasn't called. The fan is always smarter than the quarterback or the coach, or so the fan believes. Down on the sideline the coach resembles a commander in combat. He stares out at what is happening on the field while evaluating the information supplied by his aides and his troops, visualizing the game films he has studied. But the fan is always smarter, or so the fan believes.

If fans didn't think that, they wouldn't be so interested in what was happening. In a sense that too is why football is so popular.

Much of the excitement in a close game is created by the final minutes flashing away on the scoreboard clock. The referee blows his whistle. Two-minute warning. Only two minutes remain for the team that is behind, say, by four points, to score a touchdown; for the team that is behind, say, by two points, to kick a field goal. The very sight of those seconds flashing away . . . 1:59 . . . 1:58 . . . 1:57 . . . all the way down to :02 . . . :01 . . . :00 . . . creates the tension that stirs the body and soul not only of the players and coaches but also of the fans.

On the field in those last two minutes, the players and even the coaches are part of the action. The fan must suffer from a distance.

Of the major sports in America, football also is the only one that has not departed on a round-the-world trip. Baseball has been an important sport in Japan for many years. Basketball is a worldwide sport, as is ice hockey. Basketball and ice hockey are Olympic sports; baseball is expected to be an official Olympic sport in a few years after having been played at the 1984 Summer Olympic Games in Los Angeles as a "demonstration" sport. Soccer, boxing, golf, tennis, and track-and-field have long been world sports.

But except for Canada (where it's played with slightly different rules), football has remained an American sport, played by Americans (except for foreign soccer-style placekickers) for Americans.

As a result most Americans are able to identify with football players. Not that most Americans are as big or as fast as the best football players. But an American football fan may have attended the same college as his favorite wide receiver, or a fan will have grown up in the same town or area as her favorite linebacker, or a fan will root for a player simply because he is a member of that fan's favorite college team or pro team.

Football began obscurely on that field at Rutgers in 1869, developed slowly as a student activity on college campuses all over the nation, spread through the National Football League and other professional leagues into huge stadiums and onto television screens across the nation. Now, as the twenty-first century approaches, it is truly an American spectacle.

INDEX

Page references to photographs are in italic.

190

Permission for photographs is gratefully acknowledged:

NFL Properties: pp. 2 (photo: Dan Rubin), 138 (photo: Darryl Norenberg), 155 (photo: Jim Chaffin); The Bettmann Archive, Inc: p. 5; Culver Pictures, Inc: pp. 7,8; University of Chicago: p. 11; UPI/Bettmann Archive: pp. 13, 25, 40, 47, 84, 108, 118, 123, 186; Pro Football Hall of Fame: pp. 16, 19, 30, 37, 38, 42 (photo: Nate Fine), 51, 52, 54, 56, 98, 111, 142, 164, 166, 167; Archives of the University of Notre Dame: pp. 22, 27; AP/Wide World Photos: pp. 32, 45, 60, 127, 133, 144, 178, 183; Vernon J. Biever Photo: pp. 34, 67, 68, 150, 173; John E. Biever Photo: pp. 63, 71; New York Jets: pp. 73, 74 (photo: Barton Silverman), 120, 160; Baltimore Colts: p. 58; University of Alabama: p. 78; New Jersey Generals: p. 81 (photo: Jim Turner); Dallas Cowboys: pp. 85, 87, 88; Miami Dolphins: p. 91; San Francisco 49ers: pp. 94, 181; Chicago Bears: p. 103; Buffalo Bills: 106; Pittsburgh Steelers: p. 115; Los Angeles Raiders: pp. 130, 147, 176; Green Bay Packers Hall of Fame: 135; Washington Redskins: pp. 153, 156 (photo: Nate Fine).

Dave Anderson has been a sportswriter for *The New York Times* since 1966 and has been one of their "Sports of the Times" columnists since 1971. He was awarded the Pulitzer Prize in 1981 for distinguished commentary. He has written thirteen books, including the best-selling *Hey, Wait A Minute, I Wrote a Book!* which he coauthored with John Madden, football commentator and former NFL coach. In addition, he has been on the staff of the *New York Journal American* and *The Brooklyn Eagle* and has published over 300 magazine articles. Dave Anderson grew up in Brooklyn, New York and now lives in Tenafly, New Jersey with his wife, Maureen. They have four grown children: Stephen, Mark, Mary Jo, and Jean Marie.